HOW TO
HAVE YOUR CAKE AND
YOUR SKINNY JEANS TOO

Stop Binge Eating, Overeating and Dieting For Good, Get the Naturally Thin Body You Crave From the Inside Out

Josie Spinardi

Twirl Media

Cover design and interior graphics by Josie Spinardi, Taryn St. Michele and Tuck Warder
Edited by Elly Milder
Book interior and ebook by Sherry Heinitz

ISBN: 978-0-9889544-1-0

Library of Congress Cataloging-in-Publication Data is available.

Spinardi, Josie
    Thin, How to Have Your Cake and Your Skinny Jeans Too: Stop Binge Eating,
    Overeating & Dieting For Good Get the Naturally Thin Body You Crave.

Visit me on the web!
www.JosieSpinardi.com

To you.
You have hurt for too long about food.
That ends now.

TABLE OF CONTENTS

chapter one

IT'S NOT YOU! WHY DIETING HASN'T WORKED

YOU ABSOLUTELY CAN GET AND STAY THIN

I s food your best friend—and your worst enemy? Are you relentlessly bombarded by thoughts of it? Do the swirls of chocolate frosting crowning the cupcakes at your favorite café call to you from their shiny glass case? Yet at the same time, you're *painfully* dissatisfied with your current weight, your dress size constantly at the mercy of your cravings. You're exhausted from the maddening cycle. Your firm morning resolve to "be good" with food consistently crumbles into a night of takeout on the couch, watching TV with Ben & Jerry. And despite spending the vast majority of your waking hours striving to lose weight— the pounds just don't seem to budge. Do you love food, but at the same time, part of you hates it with a passion, and would be perfectly happy if you never ate again—if it just meant you could *finally* be thin?

Let me come right out and say it. *It's not you*. There are clear-cut, *solvable* reasons why your eating currently feels frustrating and at times painfully out of control. But *you* are *not* one of those reasons. You may have convinced yourself that the problem is your lack of willpower. You may secretly even fear that you're addicted to food. By the end of this chapter you will have the information you need put each of those fears to rest. For good. We'll soon be examining the overwhelming scientific evidence that dieting doesn't work to yield lasting weight loss for 99.5% of people. You are *not* alone. You are about to finally uncover the *single reason why* you've been experiencing such an uphill battle with food and your weight. And far more importantly, I am going to teach you the skills you need to win the food fight once and for all—*without dieting*.

Imagine making peace with food. Picture yourself getting and staying thin eating whatever foods you want in any situation: on vacation, at restaurants, on the go, *without* willpower—just like all of your naturally thin friends. You know, the ones who are (annoyingly) lean despite ordering whole milk in their lattes and eating *actual* lunch instead of salad with dressing on the side? Just like them, you can plan for vacations without worrying about what you'll look like in a bikini, or have dinner out with the girls without panicking on the way home about what you ate—you can even order whipped cream and chocolate drizzle on your mocha.

The skills you're about to learn are going to revolutionize your relationship with food from the inside out by addressing the *real* problem at its source. You're going to be able to lose weight *without dieting*—eating delicious, satisfying, *normal* food. Okay, this probably sounds like an outlandish claim in a world where diets are accepted as the norm—their effectiveness never being called into question. ("It's not that *the diet* failed, it was *my* lack of willpower.") But, if dieting really worked, wouldn't everyone who dieted and wanted to be thin—be thin? It's only common sense to question something that isn't working. So, that's exactly what we're going to do: evaluate the *actual effectiveness* of dieting. And we won't be using unsubstantiated claims or personal opinions. **We're about to examine a vast body of empirical scientific data spanning 70 years—from the world's leading institutions— which makes it indisputably clear that dieting is an ineffective and often painfully destructive approach to weight loss.** To better understand why the research-based skills you're about to learn are the effective solution for lasting weight loss, let's first take a closer look at what *really* happens when we diet, and identify the fundamental flaws inherent to dieting which make *any* diet destined to fail.

THE DIETING TRIANGLE OF DESPAIR

It's very likely you've already tried an assortment of diets— some sensible, some *not* so sensible. Cayenne lemonade cleanse, anyone? Chances are you've spent tons of time and energy, not to mention money, trying to get thin. You've lost weight—only to watch, (seemingly) powerless, as the pounds pile back on *every time*. If you have dieted, you're no doubt painfully familiar with "The Dieting Triangle of Despair." It goes a little something like this:

THE DIETING TRIANGLE OF DISPAIR

It starts out innocently enough. You want to lose a few pounds, so you decide to go on a diet. You read everything you can get your hands on about the diet plan. You feel powerful, in control. A wave of excitement washes over you. This time it's going to be different—this time is going to be *"it."* All you have to do is follow a few simple rules, and thinness is practically guaranteed!

You giddily clear out your cupboards, feeling a surge of hope as you toss forbidden foods and shop for new, diet-approved meals. You have an initial brilliant splash of success, and have no trouble sticking to the strict rules of your new plan. No carbs? No problem! Oil-free tuna on cardboard crackers? So worth it. You quickly lose a few pounds. People start to notice. You feel exhilarated and determined—even superior, crunching your six celery sticks spread with two teaspoons of low-fat peanut butter next to your co-worker, who's devouring a mammoth wedge of deep-dish cheese (*stuffed crust!*) pizza, oozing with mozzarella and savory aromatic toppings.

But the deprivation starts to take its toll. How long can you last? A week? A few more days? Until the waiter takes the bread basket away? Suddenly, you find yourself *freakishly aware* of what everyone around you is eating. Your boss passes your desk carrying a fresh cranberry orange muffin drenched in thick white icing. Your best friend orders seasoned curly fries with her turkey club. The guy next to you at the coffee shop takes a bite of a warm, chocolate-filled croissant and you can smell the buttery dough from four feet away. You feel the pressure starting to mount. The fearful, hungry voice deep inside starts up—quiet at first, but growing steadily louder… *You can't keep this up much longer. You just want normal food. When is it going to end? This is getting too hard!!*

Then, something happens. Your social-climbing coworker nabs the credit for a project you created. You're on the phone for forty minutes, trying to get a real human being to explain the $600 credit card charge you didn't make. Your toddler launches a sippy-cup cannon across your back seat, causing a (soon-to-be) *sour* milk explosion all over your carpet and upholstery. Whatever it is, you've reached your limit—and food is the only thing that will scratch this life-or-death-*MUST*-eat-now itch. Your resolve snaps. You eat.

This lands you face down in the second point of the triangle: the binge. Inevitably, the daily stress and demands become too great. The relentless build-up of pressure from restricting gets too intense. You've tried *so* hard, but you just can't keep it up any longer. You break your diet. And when you blow your diet, you don't just modestly nibble a couple of M&Ms. No, you devour them by the handful in savage, urgent gulps. The adrenaline pumps through your veins like a drug. In a frenzy of euphoric excitement, you sneak to the mini-mart or drive-thru and load up on chips, ice cream, fries, cookies—*anything* and *everything* that's been off-limits. The floodgates are open. You binge. Hiding in the privacy of your car or kitchen, you mentally check out and dive into the numbing sugary, salty abyss with anxious abandon. You polish off a whole bag of cookies, inhale an extra-large box of hot, grease-glistening fries, and finish it up with an entire pint of ice cream, punctuated by bites of crispy potato chips.

Ah, if only it ended there. The second your spoon hits cardboard at the bottom of the carton of Rocky Road, the fog lifts. You come to—stunned. Startled by how much you've eaten. You're even a little disoriented. And before you can get your bearings, the most ruthless of self-punishers, the Mean Girl, lashes out over the mic of your mental sound system. *I can't believe you did that! You completely blew it! You fat, disgusting pig!! You're never going to be thin!!* She is relentless. She belittles and berates you. *Nothing* is off-limits as she scathes you with her caustic commentary. The anxiety and disappointment of "blowing it" fuels the ferocity of her attack. You've eaten *so* much. You feel so powerless. So out of control.

There's only one way to satisfy the Mean Girl and stop her insult-spiked assault. You have to cut a deal—by making "the plan." Because now you have even more work ahead of you. Not only do you have the original weight to lose, you also have to make up for your little—okay, big—caloric indiscretion. You start making all kinds of promises to yourself. You'll diet more strictly, without any of that pesky moderation that may have bogged you down the last time around. No, this time you mean business. You start going free-style, creating your own damage control plan. You'll make up for all those calories by skipping breakfast. Keep lunch as light as possible. Just steamed veggies and a skinless chicken breast for dinner. You'll go to the gym after work—every night this week. Or maybe you'll go on a "cleanse"—which, let's be honest here, is really just code for not eating anything at all. You're *desperate* to make up for your slip!

You've hoisted yourself back up to the top of the triangle—determined, powerful. This time, you won't blow it. This time, you'll *make* it stick. The morning after your binge you set out to execute your plan. You skip breakfast. For lunch: seven mini caramel rice cakes and a Diet Coke. *Okay, I can do this,* you tell yourself, white-knuckling it through the three o'clock slump. But on the way home from work, traffic is intense. Some jerk has been riding your tail for miles on the freeway. You're exhausted—and, more than that, you're starving. That's when the little deprivation-driven voice kicks in again. *You've worked so hard today. You deserve something good to eat. Do it. Stop and get something. Just this once. It will taste so good. Just a few little bites. You'll be really good tomorrow.* And in an instant your plans of broiled chicken breast and steamed broccoli landslide into a hot bucket of crispy fried chicken, a giant mound of mac and cheese, and half of a still-partially-frozen cheesecake. You know what's coming next. *I can't believe you did it—again!* You whip around the triangle with the relentless fury of a bad carnival ride: diet, binge, beat yourself up. Diet, binge, beat yourself up. Over. And over. And over.

Except with each lap around the triangle, the stops get more disturbing. Your diets get stricter, your restrictions more extreme. The binges get scarier and, well… *weirder.* You find yourself standing in your kitchen, eating dry ramen noodles right out of the package. You get up in the middle of the night and eat peanut butter with a spoon straight from the jar, hunched over in the pantry. In the dark. There's a hunger inside you no amount of food is able to fill. *You are consumed by the uncontrollable urge to eat.* You live in terror, tyrannized by this unpredictable enemy that's lurking inside. You become nervous about being left alone with food, never knowing when "it" will strike. You beat yourself up more and more viciously. You're left drained, demoralized—and defeated.

What started out as an innocent attempt to lose a few pounds has spiraled out of control. You feel completely powerless. You think about food—ALL THE TIME. **Your life is being consumed by a constant and relentless inner tug-of-war between the desperate desire to lose weight, and the out-of-control drive to eat.**

Does this all sound painfully familiar? That's because these are the *proven results* of dieting.

IT'S NOT YOU!

Let me say it again: You are not alone and you are not broken. IT IS NOT YOU. It is *not* your lack of willpower. You are *not* addicted to food, or sugar, or carbs. You don't have a defective metabolism. There is actually *nothing* wrong with you. Sure, how you are currently eating might not be working for you—we *can* and *will* change that. But the vicious cycle you're trapped in, and the *reason* that your eating feels painfully out of control, is the extremely destructive—and *scientifically proven*—natural side effect of dieting.

Research shows, time and time again, that chronic dieting triggers binge eating. Dieting is the *wrong* tool for getting and staying thin. And using the wrong tool for any task can be anything from annoying to devastating. Think about trying to hammer a nail into the wall with a kitchen whisk, or the aftermath of trying to do it with a blowtorch! You're bound to feel like a total failure, but it was the *tool* that was ineffective, *not* your effort. Once you get your hands on the correct tool, a few taps, and the nail slides in almost effortlessly.

The exact same thing is true with weight loss. Once you replace dieting (the tool which is scientifically proven to result in failure for 99.5% of people), with Hunger Directed Eating (which is how naturally thin people eat and easily maintain their leanness), getting to—and staying at—your naturally thin body weight will come with ease. Why? Because now you'll be using the *right* tool.

LET'S LOOK AT THE DATA

So, maybe a part of you is still thinking…"but, *everyone* says that dieting is what you have to do to lose weight. You say it's not me, but I see advertisements of people who have lost weight and look great! If I just had more willpower, I could have success like them. Why should I believe in this approach—and not the others?" Well, if that thought has run through your mind, I'm actually delighted to hear it, because a healthy level of skepticism is just that—*healthy*. Diets are an ineffective and disastrous tool for losing weight. And it is important that you have the empirical evidence that proves it.

First off, some people do successfully lose weight from dieting—but *far* fewer than you would think. Let's take a closer look at the actual scientific data. Arthur Frank, medical director of the George Washington University Weight Management Program, reports that out of every 200 people who start a diet, only *ten* of them will successfully meet their weight-loss goals. Only ten of them! And the odds get significantly worse when you look at the long-term outcomes. Out of those ten people, only *one* of them will keep the weight off over time. ONE person. That's a failure rate of 99.5%—that's egregious. We would *never* rely on something with such dismal credentials in other areas of our lives. Let's look at this objectively. If an airline had the same track record, would you fly with them? Seriously. Out of every 200 departing flights, *one* of them lands safely? The other *199* crash and burn? *Really?* You can't tell me that you'd even *consider* flying that airline. And, if by some momentary lapse in judgment, you did fly with them and mid-flight the plane's engine cut out—would you then turn around and blame *yourself* for the malfunction?

Of course not! But that's *exactly* what we do when it comes to dieting. You embark on a journey in a vehicle that fails *199 times* out of 200—and then you beat the heck out of yourself when you don't land at your destination rocking your skinny jeans.

No, Really. Diets Don't Work: A UCLA Study

A team of experts at UCLA analyzed every study that followed dieters over a two- to five-year period. Not *some* studies. Not *most* studies. Every single published, long-term dieting study was included. The results were published in the APA journal, *American Psychologist*. When interviewed about the findings, UCLA's Tracy Mann said that the results of their data were conclusive: "Diets do not lead to sustained weight loss, or health benefits, for the majority of people." She added that most people would be "better off not going on a diet at all. Their weight would be pretty much the same, and their bodies would not suffer the wear and tear from losing weight and gaining it all back." Initially, she explained, many people lose five to ten percent of their body weight. But the *majority* of people regained *any* weight that they had lost. **So, the exhaustive review of every published long-term dieting study—by one of the leading universities in the country—found that diets are ineffective for weight loss.**

But wait. There's more.

This would be bad enough, but the news gets even worse. It turns out there is one outcome dieting consistently produces. Are you ready for it? Weight *gain*. Yes, you read that correctly. The data indicates that dieting consistently leads to **weight gain.** The UCLA team concluded that "one of the best predictors of weight gain over the four years was having lost weight on a diet at some point during the years before the study started."

Hello, talk about crash and burn! Not only do diets fail at producing (or maintaining) weight loss, but they actually make you *gain* weight? It's so bad that it's almost some kind of sick joke! That's like an acne cream that gives you cystic facial boils—or a fire alarm that doesn't work near heat or flame, and has a tendency to shoot off sparks! And the fallout from dieting just keeps coming...

Adding Insult to Injury—or, Diets Make You Fat and Crazy

I wish I could tell you that the negative effects of dieting end there. It would be one thing if diets just plain didn't work. But in addition to its abysmal failure rate, dieting is proven to make things worse—much worse. On many levels. Not only are they ineffective for long-term weight loss (and make you heavier!), but studies *also* show that dieting leads to food obsession, emotional distress, and—wait for it—*binge eating*. That's right. Dieting is scientifically proven to lead to **binge eating.** These far more insidious and long-term repercussions of dieting are best illustrated in what remains, to this day, the most definitive research on the subject: The Ancel Keys study.

THE ANCEL KEYS "SEMI-STARVATION" STUDY

Dr. Ancel Keys became well known in the 1940s for introducing K rations. Around the end of World War II, he led the first scientific study of calorie restrictions at his laboratory at the University of Minnesota. He was contracted by the War Department, which was interested in establishing a minimum amount of daily rations necessary to nourish and rehabilitate those suffering from famine in war-torn Europe. He was trying to determine the most efficient rations. In other words, at its onset, Keys' study had nothing to do with dieting.

Keys recruited four hundred men for his study. After a detailed screening, which involved rigorous psychological and physiological examinations by a team of doctors, the top thirty-six mentally and physically robust men were handpicked to participate. This elite group was chosen because they were the *most* psychologically and socially well-adjusted, active, good-humored, and motivated. And, just to ensure that the men were mentally and physically thriving—and that the initial exhaustive screening didn't miss anything—the researchers followed the men for three months before the onset of the experiment.

Then, the study began.

The men were put on what was called a "semi-starvation diet" of around 1,600 calories a day. (Okay, I know you veteran dieters are out there thinking, *1,600 calories is semi-starvation? Are you kidding me? That's what I eat on a* bad *day!*) The participants, mostly U-Minn students, went on with their lives. At first, they noticed some physical changes. They complained of feeling cold, tired, and hungry. They had trouble concentrating. Some felt dizzy. Some had headaches. But these minor discomforts were nothing compared to the *profound*—and totally unexpected—*psychological impact* of restricting their diet.

Finding #1: Increased Preoccupation With Food

One of the first significant changes that emerged was a dramatic increase in their preoccupation with food. Suddenly the men were *obsessed* with food. They talked about it. They daydreamed about it. They began to develop elaborate rituals and rules associated with mealtimes. They'd spend an inordinate amount of time planning out what they would eat and how they would distribute their calories throughout the day. They started *collecting* cookbooks. We're talking about young college men—guys with no previous unusual or particular interest in food—who are now spending every free moment ogling *Good Housekeeping* recipes. One of them collected over a *hundred* cookbooks during the course of the study. Another participant, who was interviewed years later about the study, recalled going to a movie and not even caring about the plot (or love scenes)—instead, he remembered noticing every time a character ate and every single thing they consumed. Another participant recalled that he couldn't wait for the experiment to be over. It wasn't because he was in physical discomfort. It was because the study "made food the most important thing in one's life."

In addition to the growing food fixation, the men began to demonstrate other disturbing changes in their relationship with food. One of the participants said he'd frequently go to the bakery, buy a large box of donuts, and not take a *single* bite. Instead, he would hand them out to children playing in the street—and watch, enraptured, as the kids devoured them. Initially, participants were allowed to chew gum, but Keys soon banned it when he realized some of the men were chewing up to *forty* packs a day. They began hoarding food. Sneaking food. Some even brought food into their beds at night.

These previously healthy men were suddenly *completely obsessed* with food.

Finding #2: Severe Emotional Distress

As the weeks passed, the psychological impact grew more serious. The men became tired and irritable. They lost their ambition. They began to feel inadequate. *Which makes me incredibly sad, thinking of all the women who diet hoping that they'll finally see themselves as "good enough"—when in reality, the tool they're using actually intensifies their painful sense of inadequacy.* They lost interest in their studies and their friends. They even lost their sense of humor. They became anxious, apathetic, and withdrawn. (Any of this sound familiar?) Their psych evaluations began to include findings of depression, hysteria, hypochondria, difficulty concentrating, and dramatic decreases in sex drive. The emotional distress these men experienced was so severe that two of them had stints in mental institutions, and one man even began to harm himself physically.

Finding #3: Bingeing and Self Reproach

Several of the men were unable to stick with the dietary restrictions. They weren't on lockdown, so they had access throughout the day to food that wasn't included in the study's rations. Soon, these men reported they were bingeing on vast quantities of food—followed by severe episodes of self-reproach. (*Painfully familiar!*) One man reported eating multiple ice cream sundaes and chocolate malts. Then he stole some candy. *Then* he ate several raw rutabagas. *Rutabagas. Really?* (Okay, *that* one's not so familiar.) He immediately confessed to the experimenters that he had broken the dietary rules, and then began to verbally beat up and defame himself in front of them.

Other men admitted sneaking scraps of food from garbage cans. One man "experienced serious difficulties when confronted with unlimited access to food. He repeatedly went through the cycle of eating tremendous quantities of food, becoming sick, and then starting all over again." (Yes, I'm still talking about a study. Of men. *Normal* men. In the 1940s.) Some of the men actually quit the study, because the bingeing became so frequent they were unable to continue their restricted diets and remain within the confines of the study.

They grew profoundly self-critical. And, the next part blows my mind. These previously well-balanced men began to experience *distorted body images*, and reported feeling *overweight, moody, emotional*—and *depressed.*

Please tell me you're at least *starting* to believe the problem isn't you!

Going Back To Normal

When the experiment ended—just a few months later—the men were allowed to go back to eating normally. But these poor men's eating was anything *but* normal. Many of the men had lost control of their appetites, and "ate more or less continuously." One man reported eating enormous, five-or-six-thousand calorie meals—only to start snacking again an hour later. Another man ate so much the first day after the study ended that he had to be taken to the hospital to have his stomach pumped. And another consumed so much he threw up. On a public bus. **They reported not being able to satisfy their psychological hunger no matter how much they ate.**

One of the men expressed having an inability to satisfy his craving for food simply by filling his stomach—it was *never* enough. *Oh, don't you know that feeling?* He went on what he called a year-long binge. He put on substantial weight. This man was perfectly healthy and had a normal relationship with food just *months* earlier. No longer were these the well-adjusted, good humored, motivated men that began this endeavor. Dieting had changed them—rendering them almost *unrecognizable.*

And this was a one-time experience—*not an entire lifetime of dieting.* How many of us started dieting in high school? Middle school? Today, girls are beginning to diet in *elementary school.* Here's the kicker, this study *could not* be repeated today because the American Psychological Association would forbid it for the "unethical, inhumane treatment of subjects." Keys himself admitted, when he was interviewed years later, that no other human experiment quite like it will ever be conducted again because, given what we know now, it would be seen as *too cruel* and *life threatening.* Does any of this sound familiar? Depression. Irritability. Food-obsession. An appetite that *can't* be satisfied. All topped off by savagely beating yourself up when you break the rules. **If there is one thing that we can learn from what these poor men went through, it is this: These are the natural results of dieting and food restriction.**

THE SEVEN REASONS WHY DIETS DON'T WORK

Okay, so you've seen the evidence. Dieting doesn't work. But *why?* There are seven main reasons why dieting is the wrong tool for lasting, healthy weight loss.

1. Dieting intensifies cravings and a preoccupation with food.

In reality, restricting what you eat does nothing to restrain you from eating. Instead, it only exacerbates the urge by intensifying your cravings and your focus on food. It's as if once you start dieting, your mind has switched the food radar on—you *can't stop* thinking about it. You notice food in magazines. On television. On your coworkers' desks. Suddenly, you're inexplicably aware of the exact location of every bakery within an eighteen-mile radius. You crave sweets, carbs, fats—whatever it is your diet forbids—more often, and more ferociously, than ever before. You can't even keep certain foods in your house without them calling to you from inside the cupboards.

This is *not* a sign of weakness on your part. It's simply the natural result of scarcity making something more desirable. The scarceness *itself* causes us to want it more. It's a scientifically validated fact. Marketers know it, smart girls on the dating scene know it, MAC Cosmetics knows it with their clever limited-edition collections. To this day I *still* regret not purchasing fifty tubes of their Victorian lipstick. (*Sigh.*) But somehow this fact goes out the window when we start dieting. Forbidding something dramatically fuels the desire for it. Think Romeo and Juliet, Eve and the apple—you and chocolate frosting.

A study published in the *Journal of Personality and Social*

Psychology illustrates this point beautifully. Researchers divided their participants into two groups. One group was told to picture a white bear in their minds as often as they could in a set amount of time. The other group was told *not* to think about white bears for the same amount of time. Each time participants in both groups thought about white bears, they were told to hit a buzzer in front of them. Guess which group pushed the buzzer most frequently? Yep. The people forbidden to think about white bears—they couldn't *stop* thinking about white bears. The people *encouraged* to frolic with their imaginary polar friends? Not so much.

Which makes sense. Because of the way the brain works, you have to remember what you're not supposed to think about in order to actively *not* think about it. (Okay, now my brain hurts.) The same thing happens as soon as you restrict a certain food. It becomes forbidden, and therefore thought about much *more* frequently. Which is kind of like throwing gasoline on a fire to put it out. It's liquid after all, right?

Not only does dieting nurture an obsession with food, a research team at the University of Toronto found that dieters started drooling—literally—at the mere *sight* of food. No. Seriously. When presented with food, dieting participants salivated more just looking at it than non-dieters did. It turns out restricting what you eat doesn't just effect your mental processes. It changes your actual physiological response to food. Dieting makes you physically crave it more! (This data produces the same feeling about dieting in me as when I see a car making a wrong turn onto a one-way street—I can't help but shout out *"Stop! You're going the wrong way!"*)

Think about the food that you last went overboard with. The food that sends you spinning out of control. It's probably something you routinely forbid yourself from having, right? I invite you to consider that it is not your weakness—or some kryptonite-like power the food has over you—that creates this intense response. It's the mere fact that the food is forbidden. Which leads us into the second reason why diets don't work.

2. Dieting makes you eat more, not less.

Restricting your caloric intake does change how much you eat—but *not* in the way you might think. Naturally, when you start dieting you assume you'll eat less, but the data is conclusive: dieters actually eat *more* than people who are not restricting what they eat. The rock star of international diet research, Janet Polivy, explains that for dieters, eating is marked with periods of successful abstinence, or decreased eating. But these periods are then promptly canceled out by episodes of giving in and bingeing on "forbidden" foods. (Uh, can anybody out there relate to that one?)

A 1988 study actually established a *causal relationship* between dieting and overeating. Researchers randomly assigned obese women to one of three groups: dieting, exercise only with no dietary changes, and a control group where the women changed nothing for seven weeks. Throughout the study, measurements showed that the dieters ate significantly *more* than the women in the exercise-only and control groups. The dieters would go through periods of eating less, but then overcompensate (read: binge). The result? They consumed more calories than women in both of the other groups. **It is a scientific fact: dieting causes people to overeat.**

One of the most disheartening studies illustrating this phenomenon was published in the *Journal of Consulting and Clinical*

Psychology. Researchers followed adolescent girls engaged in what they called "extreme efforts to lose weight." This included dieting, appetite suppressants, laxatives, and excessive exercise. Girls who used these methods were actually more likely to gain weight over time—and were at a higher risk for the onset of obesity than their non-dieting peers. (Heartbreaking! And exactly why it is my mission to get this information into the hands of girls *before* they're introduced to their first "gateway" diet.)

Bestselling author Geneen Roth nailed it when she said that for every diet, there is an equal opposing binge. I love that—it's *so* true. The extent and ferocity with which you binge is directly proportional to the extent to which you restrict what you eat.

3. Dieting makes you feel out of control with food.

One of the key seductive allures about dieting is its promise to bring some desperately desired order and control back to your eating. The problem is, dieting *is not* the tool to get that control. It makes perfect sense that you'd be frantically searching for a way to reclaim some authority over your relationship with food, and there are ways to get that sense of mastery and safety. But dieting is *not* it.

In fact, studies show that dieting quickly—and profoundly—causes your eating to feel *more* out of control. Just *fourteen days* of dieting is enough time to see this striking decrease in your sense of power with food. The *British Journal of Clinical Psychology* published a study of dieting men and women that highlighted this particular causal connection between dieting and feelings of control (or lack thereof). The men in the study had restricted themselves to 1,500 calories a day, and the women 1,200. The researchers monitored daily changes in their psychological state, and found that after just fourteen days into the study, participants showed a dramatic loss of control over their eating. Restricting what they ate actually *caused* them to become more powerless in restraining their eating when compared to their pre-diet test scores.

This is just one of *many* studies which support the finding that when people start dieting, they exhibit more chaotic and extreme eating patterns, and consistently report an experience of loss of control over their food intake. (And if your track record with dieting is anything like mine, I bet you don't need a study to tell you that!) So, you turn to dieting, seeking some much-needed control with food—and it disastrously backfires, causing you to feel much *more* unrestrained in your eating. You focus your energy on dieting more strictly, which only creates more intense bingeing. Then, rather than realizing the diet is to blame—you tragically turn around and beat yourself up for "blowing it."

When you diet, you are outsourcing your eating regulation to your neocortex (the part of your brain involved in voluntary self-control). Rather than letting your appetite run on autopilot in the hypothalamus where it belongs (the spot nestled in your limbic system designed to expertly regulate your hunger, thirst, pulse, blood pressure, and oxygen intake), you're routing it through a part of your brain that isn't suited to the task. Turning eating needs into (painstaking) choices that require your constant conscious control to guarantee compliance is like placing guards at the gate. If the guards are alert and well trained not a single starch gets in. But the *moment* the guards get tired, agitated, or (heaven forbid) a little tipsy, mutiny ensues—and it's carbs gone wild! That's why if you happen to have a few cocktails when you're dieting, suddenly it seems like a perfectly good idea to dive face-first into a mound of super nachos with a side of fries at 2am.

The Food-Addiction Test

Given the very rapid and forceful deterioration dieting brings to your ability to control your eating, it is perfectly understandable that you might secretly fear that maybe you're *addicted* to food. When a person's actions are *perceived* to be thoroughly out of their control, the behavior can often be labeled with a certain ominous classification: Addiction. The notion of overeating being an addiction, rather than a very strongly learned habitual response has become increasingly popular in recent years. But as indicated in the overwhelming body of scientific research that we have just explored, habitually overeating or binge eating is in fact a *very powerfully anchored* conditioned (learned) response to both dieting (food restriction) and a shortage of skills to navigate certain distressing emotional states. If you *do* secretly fear that you're addicted to food, here is a single test that can settle that internal (frightening) debate—*once and for all*.

Have you ever had one of those clandestine eating episodes where you felt momentarily alone and were sneaking food—maybe you were standing in someone's kitchen at a party or holiday gathering, or were in a break room at work eating some communal food that was sitting out—and even though a huge part of you *really* wanted to stop (and was terrified of being seen), no amount of pep talk you could give yourself in that moment would talk you off the ledge? The pull was too strong. That buzzy, "binge-y" feverishness was taking over. You were going for it—future thinness (and bikini) be damned! And *as* you were shoving more of whatever you were eating into your mouth— someone you respected, or didn't know very well (or worse yet had a crush on!) walked into the room. (Oh. The. *Horror*.) What did you do? You stopped eating. Right? And in fact, I'll venture to guess that no amount of money could have enticed you to continue the frantic consumption that felt so completely inescapable just seconds before the person walked in. Well, if you were truly "addicted," powerless, or suffering from an overriding physical chemical dependence on that food—your biggest celebrity crush walking into the room still wouldn't be enough to get you to stop.

And yet, YOU DID STOP. So, *why* were you able to stop? Because in that moment, the desire to not be seen eating in that *more private* way was a stronger motivation than the pull to eat. Plain and simple. So, you can now take great relief in knowing, once and for all, that you are *not* addicted to food. The nutty (and painful) eating behaviors you may currently be experiencing are very normal responses to deprivation. The skills you're going to learn in this book will put you back in the driver's seat with your eating, giving you the sense of mastery and control that you've been longing for.

4. Dieting increases both emotional distress and the likelihood that you'll eat in response to the stress.

This is the ultimate one-two punch. Remember those poor starvation study participants? Those strapping, good-humored guys who went from well adjusted to total trainwrecks? Not only does dieting cause (and amplify) feelings of emotional distress, it dramatically increases the likelihood that you will *eat* in response to those painful emotions when they arise. In 1995, Jane Ogden of Kings College in London found that food restriction increased depression, anxiety, guilt, and feelings of powerlessness. Dieting not only negatively impacted a participant's mood, it significantly affected their motivation in general. Not just in food- or weight-related areas—in *all* areas of their lives. Again, these disturbances manifested just weeks after beginning the diet.

Another study at the University of Hertfordshire showed participants images of either food or non-food objects. When these female dieters looked at pictures of chocolate, their levels of anxiety, guilt, and depression shot through the roof. They didn't even get the momentary pleasure of *eating* the chocolate for their trouble! Just *looking* at pictures of it reduced them to nervous, depressed, guilt-ridden messes. Who needs that?

Let's take a look at the second blow of this one-two punch— that dieting increases the likelihood you'll eat in response to emotional distress. First off, stress eating goes against your body's built-in physiological response. It's actually *un*natural to eat in response to stress. You see this in all your naturally thin friends, right? As soon as their life gets tense, their jeans start falling off their bodies. That's because stress activates the autonomic nervous system, which in turn elevates your blood sugar levels and decreases hunger. It's part of that whole "fight or flight" instinct designed to preserve us and keep us alive. Think about it. You're out in the wild and a tiger starts chasing you—you're *not* going to pull over and order a Big Mac. Of course not! Your body shuts down hunger when stress occurs so you can focus all of your energy on survival.

Many of the factors that trigger overeating in dieters actually inhibit eating in non-dieters. For example, non-dieters eat less than they normally would if they're anxious, distressed, or depressed. But research shows that dieters tend to *overeat* when they're upset. This is the result of learned helplessness—a very specific Non-Hunger Eating response to stress that I call Licking Your Wounds. (More about that in Chapter 2.)

5. Dieting creates a whole new category of overeating called "Eating Cuz You Ate."

You know how it is. You go a little overboard on dinner. Or eat a couple of the kids' off-limits Oreos. *Ah, what the heck,* you think. *I've already blown it.* So you do the *only* logical thing in response— you finish the entire package. Right? And you continue eating directly through to your next official starting point. Which could be tomorrow, or Monday morning, or… New Year's Day.

Oops.

Studies show that when individuals start eating by external rules and restrictions (a.k.a. dieting), the likelihood that they'll overeat in response to breaking a rule skyrockets. **Once you start eating according to arbitrary rules, you can only ever be in one of two possible states at any given time: on your diet, or breaking your diet.** Right? Not only does this dichotomy reinforce "all-or-nothing" thinking—a key factor in binge eating—it sets you up to trigger the second type of Non-Hunger Eating: Eating Cuz You Ate. Which can instantly turn one tiny, 50-calorie slip-up into an three-hour, 2,450-calorie binge.

Sure, that sounds crazy. But it makes sense. Think about it. You've been plugging along, sticking to the strict (let's face it—*miserable*) guidelines of your diet. Your guards are rocking their posts at the gate, only allowing you boneless, skinless chicken breast and steamed spinach for weeks. And then that coworker down the hall brings cake in for her birthday. Not just any cake. Decadent, moist, creamy chocolate ganache cake. You've been so good—maybe just that tiny corner piece with the little pink frosting flower... And it tastes unbelievable. The flavor explodes in your mouth. Rich, intense, chocolaty goodness. And in the explosion the floodgates burst open, the guards are knocked out. *Gone.* You eat like there's no tomorrow.

Because for you, there *is* no tomorrow when it comes to food that actually tastes *this* good. You'll be back to rice cakes and water and hours on the treadmill just to make up for the cake—*and* all that you inhaled in its aftermath. *What the heck*, you figured. Might as well go all-out on the way home. Pizza? Pint of Häagen-Dazs? Half the takeout Chinese menu? The damage is already done. That's how a single small divergence from your diet plan explodes into a full-force binge.

I joke about it—but bingeing in response to a tiny diet "infraction" can land you in an incredibly painful and demoralizing place. You feel *so* discouraged. You've blown it. *Again.* The hope of doing better tomorrow gets dimmer and dimmer as your slip-ups grow more frequent, and your rebound eating begins to span several days. This pattern isn't unique to dieting—bingeing in response to breaking a rule happens with alcohol, cigarettes, heroin, cocaine, shopping, gambling. It has nothing to do with food specifically. It's the *direct result* of using abstinence and restraint as a means of behavioral change.

6. Diets don't model naturally thin eaters' behavior.

Have you ever noticed how your naturally thin friends eat? You know, the friends who never diet. They're not skinny because they obsess over food. They use regular salad dressing, and don't bother with nonfat yogurt. They'll eat the bagels and donuts other people bring into the office. They're not lean because of their extensive knowledge of nutritional data. They don't have a clue how many calories are in a slice of bread, let alone the carb-to-protein ratio of their favorite lunchtime sandwich, or what a carb is exactly—and why they are to be feared so greatly!

Think about it. If you want to learn how to do something, isn't it just common sense to copy someone who does it really, really well? If you want to play tennis, you study Serena Williams. Want to build a multi-million dollar empire without a college degree? Read up on Richard Branson. But dieting in no way, shape, or form resembles how naturally thin people eat or interact with food. In fact, the two approaches differ in almost *every single aspect*.

What they eat: Naturally thin eaters don't drink diet soda, they don't eat fat-free cookies, or low carb anything—and they never order their toast "dry." They take a very straightforward approach toward food. Generally, they just eat what they like when they're hungry. (Crazy, right?)

How they eat: Remember the last time you had dinner with your naturally skinny friend? "I'm starving!" she exclaimed, poring over the menu. For you: The (*boring*) garden salad, of course. Low-fat vinaigrette, on the side. For her: The spinach ravioli in lemon cream sauce. "How can you stand to eat that rabbit food?!" she asked incredulously, eyeing your plate. Which did look pretty sad next to her puffy pasta pillows of ricotta, swimming in creamy, lemon-y deliciousness. While you resigned yourself to your salad, she dove in. "This is so good!" she declared. And then a few minutes later, after just twelve bites, she did the unthinkable—she *stopped* eating.

Because she was full.

When they eat: Naturally thin people eat when they're hungry and stop when they're full. They don't eat because the clock says it's lunchtime, or they're home alone and don't know what to do with themselves. They don't eat to distract themselves from their loneliness, or because they just ate two mini Snickers bars so they might as well polish off the whole bag. And if they do go a little overboard and eat until they're stuffed, they don't say, *Oh well, there goes that*, and keep eating long past the point where they've overdone it. No, they simply feel physically uncomfortable—and wait *until they're hungry* before they eat again.

Many years ago—while I was still in the midst of my struggle with food—I had a conversation with a naturally thin friend of mine that I'll *never* forget. I had just experienced a particularly intense overeating episode, and was feeling utterly distraught and depressed. I was trying to describe to him how I was feeling, but was in such a low place that I couldn't even put into words the anguish I was in. "I can't even explain it," I told him. "I just feel so… so…"

"Full?" he interjected.

Worthless? Miserable? Ashamed? Definitely. But *full*? Full had never even *occurred* to me as a way to describe how I felt. I was so focused on my feelings of guilt and shame that I was totally in my head—not registering what was *physically* happening in my body at all. That moment was a total revelation for me. Naturally thin eaters are aware of what's actually happening in their physical bodies. If they eat past the point of being full—and sometimes they do—they recognize that it doesn't feel good to be overstuffed. They make a mental note not to do it again. And they move on. End of story. They don't feel demoralized. They don't come up with some elaborate, lofty plan that will make up for their massive moral failing. They don't tell themselves that they're disgusting failures who are destroying their only chance at having a happy life. They just wait until they feel hungry again. And then they eat.

7. Diets do not resolve the real reasons you eat when you're not hungry.

Let's be honest here: There are a lot of reasons why we eat, and hunger is just one of them. The final reason why diets don't work for long-term weight loss is they do absolutely nothing to deal with the *real* reasons why you would ever eat when you're not physically hungry. And they definitely don't equip you to resolve those reasons. Somehow it has become widely accepted that food is the problem, for which calorie restriction is the solution. Not only is dieting the wrong tool, it's not even addressing the *real* problem—*why* you eat when you're not hungry.

Essentially, a diet is just a set of rules. Knowing how many calories you're "allowed" to eat in a day does not endow you with the ability to stay under that limit. And having a list that tells you what you can and can't eat does *absolutely nothing* to enable you to stick to that list. We all know that telling yourself what you should and shouldn't eat once you get to *"that place"* right before a binge is about as effective as standing in the path of a speeding locomotive, shouting "Stop! Stop! No, really! Stop!!" You can *want* to be thin more than anything else in the world. You can make a serious, earnest commitment to lose weight. But making a commitment doesn't mean that you have the capacity to carry it through. There's a whole different skillset that will enable you to create new habits and implement behavior changes that go far beyond willpower and "just say no."

Diets address the symptom, not the root problem. Diets deal with limiting calories, or changing the types of foods you eat. Replacing nachos with carrots sticks *doesn't do anything* to address the reasons *why* you're eating when you're not hungry. Why you feel hungry all the time. Or why certain foods seem to have such a kryptonite-like power over you—to the point that you can't even be alone in the same room with them without going crazy.

Using diets to lose weight does *nothing* to resolve the real underlying issues. It's like taking aspirin to treat strep throat. It will mask the symptoms for a while, bring your fever down, maybe even make your throat feel a little better, but it doesn't do a thing to address the real root cause of your pain. You need a different treatment—the right tools—to resolve that problem at its source. Dieting might temporarily treat the symptom… if you're lucky. But, as we've seen, it actually *intensifies* the underlying problem, triggering both Gasping for Food and Eating Cuz You Ate. Not only does dieting fail to eliminate overeating, it actually makes the problem *worse*, and more complex.

EXTREME MAKEOVER:
THE TRUTH CHANGES EVERYTHING

Knowledge is power. Now that you've examined the empirical data that proves diets do *not* lead to lasting weight loss—and we've walked through numerous studies establishing the fact that dieting leads to *binge eating, weight gain,* and some serious *emotional* and *psychological distress*—you are in a powerful place. You are now in the position to see this challenge in a completely different light.

You haven't failed at dieting—*dieting* has failed *you*.

chapter two

THE REAL PROBLEM —AND ITS SOLUTION

How to Stop Non-Hunger Eating for Good:
The Root Cause Analysis of Binge Eating,
Overeating & Emotional Eating

FINALLY, THE REAL (SOLVABLE) REASON WHY YOU'VE BEEN STRUGGLING WITH FOOD

So, let's recap. We spent Chapter 1 looking at the hard data that proved diets don't work for 99.5% of people for lasting weight loss—and, oh yeah, that's right—they cause a whole mess of other painful problems. Great! Nobody really wants to be on a diet all the time, anyway. Agreed? But, if dieting doesn't work… how the heck *do* you lose weight?

In the last chapter we uncovered why dieting is the wrong tool for weight loss—and therefore not the *real* solution. Even with this knowledge, it's tempting to think that *the excess weight* is still the real problem. Especially if you've spent years trying to get thin. But the fact is, extra weight is just a symptom—a byproduct of the real problem. You've been spending all of your energy trying to clean up the puddle on the floor, that just keeps returning. Instead, let's fix the leak in the roof.

In this chapter we'll dismantle some diet myths that may be holding you back, and take a closer look at the *real*, definable, (solvable) underlying behaviors, beliefs, and habits that are driving us to eat in a way that creates excess weight.

CARBS, FAT, AND YOUR METABOLISM ARE NOT THE PROBLEM

According to diet-logic, fat, carbs, and simple sugars are the three things between you and the jeans you haven't been able to fit into in years. But, wait a minute. We all have those naturally thin friends that eat hot dogs and giant soft pretzels at the ballpark, or enjoy regular soda and buttered popcorn at the movie theater. They're still able to effortlessly (*annoyingly*) maintain their naturally lean weight, despite eating "fattening" foods. So, it *can't* just be the food. Let's start by debunking two of the most widely accepted diet-logic myths. One: *Certain foods are fattening.* Two: *A slow metabolism will make you gain weight.*

1. There is no such thing as a fattening food.

"So, are you actually, seriously trying to tell me that I can eat banana cream pie and it won't be routed directly to my thighs?" Yes, I actually, seriously am. No single food—or food group, for that matter—has the ability to cause your body to gain or store weight. Sure, some foods are more calorically dense than others, but a higher number of calories per gram just means that a food has more potential fuel, or energy. If you're listening to your body, eating only when you're hungry and stopping when you're satisfied, eating a high-calorie food just means you'll feel full a lot sooner. With a lot less food. You'd have to eat an entire vat of cabbage soup, for example to feel as full as you would from a few bites of a hearty, vegetable lasagna. The soup isn't righteous, the lasagna isn't "fattening"—they just simply provide different concentrations of body-fueling energy (calories) per bite. So a pound of carrots contains the same amount of calories as an ounce of peanuts. The *only* way either of these foods can cause your body to store fat is if you eat more of them than you use for fuel.

Robert Crayhon, MS, CN—called "one of the top ten nutritionists in the country," by *Self* magazine—puts it like this: "Choosing food by its fat and calorie content is like choosing your friends by IQ and income levels. You choose your friends because of their overall effect on your life, not their salary." Well, so it is with food. In fact, when 26,473 Americans were studied, it was found that those who ate the most nuts were the least obese. Nuts are packed with calories—in fact, they're almost pure fat. So if it were true that high-fat ("fattening") foods made you fat, the people who ate the most nuts would be the *most* obese, not the *least*.

2. A slow metabolism does not make you heavier—but it could save you money!

It's tempting then, to blame your weight loss woes on metabolism. Maybe you believe that you've been cursed with a slow metabolism—while your naturally thin friends, who can eat anything they want and stay lean, must have won the metabolism lottery. But metabolic rate isn't the problem either. If you're concerned that a slow metabolism is making you heavy, I have some great news. A slow metabolism will *never* make you heavier—it'll simply make you hungry *less* often.

Let's say you give the same 500-calorie burger to Fast Metabolism Girl, and her friend with the slower metabolic rate. Fast Metabolism Girl's body will speedily burn through her burger in a couple of hours, and then politely send a request for more fuel. Whereas, when Slow Metabolism Girl eats that same burger (off the *same* menu), her body will slowly… putter… through… the fuel, not needing more food for five or even six hours. So, if you're eating when you're hungry, and stopping when you're satisfied, a slow metabolism cannot *ever* make you gain weight. It simply means that you'll be hungry less often and your body will require less food. So hey, if your metabolism is slower—just think of all the food money you'll have leftover that you can *now spend* on shoes.

THE SINGLE CAUSE OF WEIGHT GAIN

It's mathematically *impossible* for a certain food—or a specific metabolism—to make you gain weight. There is only one reason why your body will *ever* store excess fat, and it's not exactly rocket science. (Drum roll!) It's simply that you take in more calories than your body needs for fuel. That's it. Weight gain—and weight loss, for that matter—is just simple math. The only way to gain weight is to take in more calories than your body needs. The surplus gets stored in your hips and thighs for later. And the *only* way you can overfuel your body is by Non-Hunger Eating: starting to eat when you're not physically hungry and / or eating beyond being comfortably satisfied. So if it's that simple, why would you ever eat when you weren't physically hungry?

WHY ON EARTH WOULD I EAT IF I'M NOT HUNGRY?

So, why would otherwise brilliant, sane, successful people eat when they aren't physically hungry? Two reasons.

Behind door number one—behold the Dr. Jekyll and Mr. Hyde-like eating pattern that is able to derail your thinness goals in a single bound (or bite)—the natural, scientifically validated direct response to dieting. As we've already examined in Chapter 1, restrictive, rules-based eating sets you up to for diet-induced Non-Hunger Eating. In a nutshell: dieting overrides your hunger and satiety signals, and causes you to obsess over and crave food when you are not physically hungry, and it throws in the fabulous parting gift of inciting a food riot (binge) when you break a single diet rule.

Behind door number two? Cupcake coping. The second reason you'd ever eat when you aren't hungry—is to change the way you feel. People turn to emotional eating because, let's face it, food does a pretty amazing job at changing your emotional state. Sure, eating doesn't actually change anything about your stressful situation. But when you pop the lid on that carton, in "those moments" it sure feels like Häagen-Dazs is a viable solution to 97% of the problems life throws at you. If only it didn't have that pesky little side effect of maximizing the size of your stomach and thighs. There is nothing inherently wrong, weak, or immoral about using food to change the way you feel. The problem? This mood-altering strategy greatly undermines your *other* goals: like looking great in a pencil skirt—or solving the problem that has you stressed out in the first place.

We've all been there. Pretty much everyone, at some point, has used food and the ritual of eating to escape, soothe, or just distract themselves from otherwise uncomfortable or unpleasant emotions. (I can't believe I got a parking ticket—ooh, a cookie!) This truly is the epitome of adding insult to injury. The very thing we are using to feel better (food), not only fails to have any (lasting) positive effect on the pain that spurred its use—it results in excess weight which becomes the source of its own consuming emotional anguish.

ROOT CAUSE ANALYSIS:
HOW WHAT I LEARNED IN I.T. CAN MAKE YOU THIN

So, the problem is *not you*. And the problem is *not food*. The real problem is the *learned* habit of overriding your body's internal signals for hunger and fullness. That's the behavior we want to eliminate, and to do that—we need to identify its root cause. When you know exactly why you are periodically disconnecting from hunger and fullness and using food for non-fuel purposes, you can then implement targeted solutions that resolve the problem—at its source. When you diet, you address the symptoms (overeating and excess weight). This is like going into the garden and trimming the weeds. Grueling, tedious, and ultimately futile. Because without removing the source, the problem keeps coming back. In contrast, if you pull that bugger out by the root—it's gone. For good!

Root cause analysis (RCA) is a structured problem-solving process that uncovers the multi-dimensional causes of undesirable events, so that targeted corrective measures can be taken. This process uniquely identifies the impact of hidden causes, rather than merely exploring the factors that are readily apparent.

RCA was created by Sakichi Toyoda, founder of Toyota Industries—who *Forbes Magazine* ranks as the 13th most influential businessman of all time and is often compared to Thomas Edison for his industry-redefining inventions. Toyoda developed a unique system to identify the (often inconspicuous) source of a problem, then implement solutions that prevent the problem from recurring. It was originally applied in the field of engineering, but has since been widely adopted in many industries. I became acquainted with this methodology as a strategy to find corporate solutions, back in my days as a Senior Database Architect. And upon first introduction, the psychologist in me instantly recognized its potential value in dealing with the cream cheese danish in my left hand. And the rest—was history.

This "Josie Method" is the result of my decade-long (extensive) research-based Non-Hunger Eating Root Cause Analysis. Through my research, I identified five distinct drivers of Non-Hunger Eating. But what's far more exciting (and useful) is that I devised, and tested, targeted solutions for each of the five causes—resolving, and ultimately eliminating, Non-Hunger Eating at its source.

Not all Non-Hunger Eating is alike; there are two unique types: diet-induced eating, and using food to change how you are feeling emotionally. Once you identify the underlying behaviors (dieting and emotional regulation) that drive Non-Hunger Eating—and learn the strategies to resolve their root causes—there will simply be nothing left to prompt you to reach for food when you're not hungry. You won't need willpower. You won't need rules. And you won't need to starve yourself. You just need the right tools to get to—and stay at—your naturally lean body weight.

Gasping for Food is responsible for the most frequent, violent, and out-of-control binges. My clients find it *much* easier to eliminate the more nuanced Emotional Eating behaviors once the Gasping is addressed and out of the way—whether they suffered from *small* (but still debilitating) frequent slip-ups, or *huge* demoralizing middle-of-the-night 7,000-calorie mini-mart sprees. Though this book details the solution for the first type of Non-Hunger Eating, diet-induced Gasping for Food, I've included an overview of the Emotional Eating drivers as well. I broke them down into four subgroups to give you even more clarity.

WAIT, IF YOU HAVE CREATED THE SOLUTION FOR BINGE EATING AND EMOTIONAL EATING WHY AREN'T THEY BOTH IN THIS BOOK?

Excellent question.

It's a terrible feeling to think that maybe you're being scammed or hooked by some self-serving marketing ploy—or worse yet, that someone might be *purposely* withholding information that can help you. Your trust is important to me, so I want to take a minute to give you the back-story as to *why* I released the Binge Eating Solution while the Emotional Eating Solution was still being written (rather than waiting to publish them both at the same time).

So here's the deal.

I completed and released an earlier audio version of this Gasping for Food Solution content to a small yet internationally diverse sample of people (a few hundred women and a smattering of brave men, in 18 countries, ages ranging from 13-64 years old), and I was *blown away* by the positive responses that poured into my inbox. I consistently received two and three page emails from people expressing their heartfelt gratitude for the never before experienced hope and freedom they now possessed in their relationship with food. They reveled in being free from the tyranny of bingeing after years of struggle, and giddily described the "real" foods they ate while the pounds started to fall away.

As you could imagine, this feedback was thrilling to hear— but with these cheerful notes were letters of a more serious nature. A heartbreaking number of women and men candidly shared that they found this book when they were drowning in *extremely debilitating distress* from their out-of-control relationship with food, and that the information and skills it offered equipped them to come up for air from the anguish and hopelessness and swim safely to shore.

To be clear, from a root cause analysis standpoint Binge Eating and Emotional Eating are very different behaviors, each with unique causes and distinct solutions. In fact Emotional Eating itself has three different sub-causes and corresponding skills for resolution. But the fact that they have different causes and solutions is not the reason I decided to release the solution sets sequentially. The reasons are: A) I had in my possession a completed book proven to help people in debilitating pain; I wanted you to have access to it—today. B) As mentioned above, the techniques to end emotional eating are quite different from those used to resolve binge eating (not surprising). I am designing an Emotional Eating program that captures the unique interactive elements that have been transformational for my coaching clients, so I can deliver them to you in the format that will bring you the most success.

I hope this gives you insight into why the Binge Eating and

Emotional Eating Solutions are separate entities. But far more importantly, I hope you now have clarity about my motive. My desire is to help every single person who hurts with food obtain the skills to enjoy mastery and ease in this area—as fast and effectively as humanly possible! (If you'd like info about the Emotional Eating Solution simply send a blank email to emo@josiespinardi.com, and I'll notify you by email the instant the solution is available.)

Ok now back to our regularly scheduled program…

THE FIVE TYPES OF NON-HUNGER EATING

1. Gasping for Food

If you've read this far, you're already very familiar with this one. Gasping for Food is your body's natural—and scientifically proven—response to deprivation. When you forbid yourself something you really, really want, you set yourself up to go overboard when you eventually let yourself have it.

It's like holding your breath while swimming. When you swim underwater—you're literally restricting your consumption of oxygen. Let's say you swim the full length of an Olympic-size pool, holding your breath the entire time. When you finally reach the other side and come up for air, are you going to take a teensy, delicate inhalation? No way! You're going to heave, and gasp, and gulp for air. And even after you've gotten enough oxygen to satisfy your lungs, you'll still be panting for minutes—overindulging in oxygen—until you feel psychologically assured that you're going to have ongoing, unrestricted access to air.

Well, so it is with food. Think about your own eating patterns. The foods you're most likely to overeat and feel the most out of control with—are the *exact* foods you've previously forbidden. Aren't they? This is because the second you "slip" and let yourself have them, you eat like there's no tomorrow because, quite frankly, there *will* be no tomorrow with this food—because the next morning, you'll be back to cucumbers and cottage cheese.

As you've seen, this type of overindulgence is the perfectly *normal* response to deprivation. It is proven in study after study after study. The source of this problem is *not* your lack of willpower—the problem is that banning foods is a catastrophically ineffective solution to Non-Hunger Eating. It turns a problem into a full-blown disaster!

What *is* the right solution, then? Hunger Directed Eating (HDE) is the tested, targeted (real) solution to Gasping for Food. HDE is what reconnects you with your body's natural thin-telligence: its signals of hunger and satisfaction—that expertly guide you to eat only what's right for *your* body. And just to be clear, this is not about only eating certain "healthy" foods. What's "right" for your body includes what is right for the *whole* person that inhabits it—and sometimes the "right" thing for that person in that moment is chocolate!

Hunger Directed Eating enables you to eat according to your physical and psychological needs. To identify (and eat) what you really, *really* want. (The fun part!) To be present—so you can maximize satisfaction and thoroughly enjoy each meal. To stop eating when you feel comfortably satisfied. (Which, I know, sounds *far* easier said than done right now!) And to check in and notice how various foods fuel you, so you can make adjustments from the inside out, based on how the food actually makes you feel.

I will teach you to implement the step-by-step, hands-on techniques that will allow you to *master* these skills. Eating in alignment with your body's authentic needs will soon become your natural inclination. Naturally thin eating will become your knee-jerk response. By eliminating diet-driven deprivation and stripping kryptonite foods of their current magnetic pull, you will effectively eliminate the triggers for Gasping for Food—at the root.

2. Eating Cuz You Ate

So, you're going along on your diet, and you are rocking it. Not a single carb has passed your lips for weeks—until you buy the package of Thin Mint Girl Scout cookies from your niece. They look so good. And it's been *forever* since you've had them. The minty dark chocolate wafers begin calling to you from their signature green box. Soon, your resolve begins to crumble, like—well, like a cookie. "Maybe I'll just have *one*," you tell yourself. "I've been doing so well, a single, tiny, little cookie won't hurt," you rationalize. OK, it's decided then! You excitedly tear open the cardboard seam of the box flap and pull out the translucent tray, ripping open the thin plastic encasing them—and at long last, you eat one. Nothing has *ever* tasted so good. Heaven. Euphoria. Pure, unadulterated bliss. They taste *amazing*—so you pop a few more of the neatly stacked chocolaty circles into your mouth. The slash in the cellophane protecting the cookies splits lower and lower. You're in heaven—*until*—the nagging realization of what you've just done pierces your consciousness. *Oh no! I've blown it!!* Disappointment and fear come crashing down on you. And in that same moment, a tsunami-like current pulls you forward, toward the cookies. You *really* want MORE. Your mind darts nervously between the plan it's quickly concocting to undo the caloric damage (thus far, relatively minor)—and the 23 remaining Thin Mints enticingly looking up at you. Then diet-logic kicks in. Well, you've already blown your *entire* diet by eating those five cookies, right? (Not right!) So, you may as well do the *only logical thing in response* and finish that sleeve. And before you know it—you've polished off the entire package.

At this point you figure you're already so deep over your head in excess calories that the strict deprivation you'll have to endure to repair this damage is going to be grueling. So you might as well keep eating the good stuff straight through to your next official starting point. Right? (No!) Because, as we all know, it's impossible to recover from a diet slip-up right there in the moment. No, you have to "wait" until you have the chance for a formal "fresh start." Maybe it will be tomorrow. Maybe it will be Monday morning. Or, maybe it will be New Year's Day. Oh, and by "wait," I mean "eat everything that has been off-limits with dam-bursting fervor"—*naturally*.

This is the type of Non-Hunger Eating I like to call Eating Cuz You Ate. You break one of your diet rules and figure: "What the heck, I've already blown it—I may as well just keep eating."

If you tried to explain this line of reasoning to a non-dieter, it would sound... well, insane. But every single (otherwise right-minded), successful, and fully functional client I have ever had—from Oxford to Ottawa—initially responds this same painful way to blowing her diet. And, it turns out this lunacy also holds up in the lab. So what gives?

A seminal study published in 1999 by Janet Polivy and Peter Herman asked both dieters and non-dieters to taste-test three flavors of ice cream. The dieters and non-dieters were each split into three subgroups. Prior to tasting the ice cream, the first subgroup was given *two* milkshakes to drink, the second group *one* milkshake. The third group *didn't* get a milkshake. Then, the researchers left *each* participant *alone* in a room to sample and rate the flavors of three *enormous* platters of ice cream, inviting them to eat as much as they liked.

The non-dieters ate as diet-logic would dictate: Non-dieters who *didn't* have a milkshake ate the *most* ice cream, and those who'd downed *two* milkshakes ate the *least*. They'd already consumed their body weight in ice cream—they were *full*, for heaven's sake!

The dieters, however, did the *exact opposite*. Dieters who hadn't had a milkshake ate the least ice cream. They hadn't blown their diet with the milkshake; they were still being "good." The dieters who'd already had two milkshakes? They ate the *most* ice cream of all.

The milkshake appetizer had a very different effect on dieters and non-dieters. Why? Non-dieters are regulating what they eat using their natural, internal cues for hunger and satiety. When faced with mounds of ice cream and they felt full, they simply didn't want the ice cream. Sounds perfectly reasonable, right? But dieters rely on external rules, willpower, and the most fatal regulator of all, diet-logic—rather than using their body's own signals of physical need to guide what they eat.

Dieters who *didn't* drink a milkshake were still on the wagon. With their restraint *fully intact*, they had no trigger for Eating Cuz You Ate. Whereas the dieters who drank *one* or *two* milkshakes, figured "What the heck, I've *already* blown it, I may as well keep eating until it's time to climb *back on* the wagon."

When you rely on external forces to restrain your calorie consumption, a small slip tends to lead to a prolonged period of unrestrained eating. The dieters had multiple factors working against them. Not only did they lack access to their internal fullness signals, but on top of that they suffered the painful emotions of guilt, disappointment, and anxiety about breaking their diet. Which leads to our next type of Non-Hunger Eating—the Mean Girl Munchies.

3. The Mean Girl Munchies

Take the rigid demands of perfectionism. Add a heightened sensitivity to the (real or perceived) appraisals of others. Mix in a healthy dose of harsh self-criticism. What do you get? The perfect recipe for the Mean Girl Munchies.

In this flavor of Non-Hunger Eating, food is used as a way to press mute on the tyrannical Mean Girl chatter. Who is the Mean Girl? She's the relentless voice that demands perfection and beats you up whenever you slip up—with food, with exercise, with *whatever.* She berates you for even the smallest blunder. And she's vicious. When you're given a project at work that's outside your comfort zone—*You're going to blow this,* she blasts, *you never get anything right. It won't be good enough. This time, you'll probably lose your job!* And she just doesn't quit. Cue the escape vehicle: Food. Your shoulders are tense, you're hunched over as you munch a bag of pretzels with rapid-fire repetition, staring glossy-eyed at your computer screen. The methodic rhythm of your chewing is oddly soothing. Mean Girl Munchies fare is usually bite-sized and crunchy—nothing drowns out the voice in your head like crunchy mouthfuls of pretzels, popcorn, or M&M's. Since the goal is to zone out, the Mean Girl Munchies are often paired with watching mindless TV. (Or those internet searches that land you on videos involving smoky eye tutorials or cats playing keyboards.)

The Mean Girl's harsh, critical attacks send you running for refuge—and focusing on food regulates your mood using the same strategy as (surprisingly enough) *meditation*. A 1991 study conducted by Harvard University found that **binge eating is motivated by a desire to escape from critical self-awareness**. So, to silence the Mean Girl's ruthless diatribe you narrow your attention to a solitary object or function. In meditation you might focus on your breathing. With Mean Girl Munchies, you hone in on the bright orange Cheetos. Same difference. Well, *kind of*.

And the food doesn't even have to be appealing. Researcher Janet Polivy's 1994 study found that when stressed, dieters ate food to self-regulate regardless of how bad it tasted. They ate just as much unpalatable food as delicious. The flavor was not the motivating factor—they just wanted to drown out their anguish from the Mean Girl's attack. The good news is that with a little psychological judo, you can actually turn the Mean Girl into a mentor.

4. Licking Your Wounds

Have you ever noticed how people often respond to the same obstacles in very different ways? Some people immediately start brainstorming ways over, around, or straight through them (or even negotiate deals to sell the encumbrance for parts). While others collapse in despair and give up—right from the get-go. Years ago, I stumbled across a study that completely changed the way I related to food (and challenges!). Sonja Stroop and her team found that people who did *not* emotionally eat did *one thing* differently than people who used food to cope with emotional distress. A *single* coping behavior made the difference between not using food—and using it. As if that weren't amazing enough, the people who did this one magical behavior enjoyed higher life satisfaction, attained more personal success, had more satisfying relationships and suffered from far fewer mental and physical illnesses. Whereas the people who lacked this specific skill frequently suffered from depression, anxiety, struggled with drugs, alcohol, gambling, anorexia, and bulimia. What's the million-dollar difference?

When faced with a stressor, the "Shiny Happy People" (the non-food-users) engaged in **task-oriented coping**. They took direct action to resolve, mitigate, or eliminate stressors. They focused on solving. Conversely, the people who *did* use food engaged in **emotion-oriented avoidant coping** behaviors. These people were much more likely to think that they were unable to mitigate a stressor, and as a result, focused on soothing themselves—with food. Since they (often falsely) believed that they could not change the *situation*, they focused their efforts on minimizing the distress they experienced in response to the stressor—they tried to change their *feelings*.

This is found to be true for people who use drugs, alcohol, gambling, or Nordstrom's to cope with difficult situations. If you believe there's nothing you can do to eliminate what's causing you pain, you're going to (understandably) try to alleviate the pain instead. Consequently, for a lot of people, that's where food comes in.

But why? Why do some people turn to emotional eating when faced with a tough situation, while others power through? It's simple. They really, truly believe they have no power to control—or even influence—the outcome of what is causing them distress. This cognitive powerless belief pattern is closely tied with depression. It is a phenomenon known as "learned helplessness."

Okay, brace yourself, this next experiment is heart wrenching.

In the late 1960s, researcher Martin Seligman was an assistant in a psychological study that put dogs in an enclosed pen and administered electric shocks. This pen had high walls that the dogs could not get over. At first, as you can imagine, the dogs did everything they could to escape the pain, but were not able to get over the high walls of the pen. And eventually, they stopped resisting. They stopped trying to escape. They learned that no matter what they tried, they were unable get away—that nothing they could do would allow them to avoid the shocks. Later, the same dogs were put in a different pen that again administered electric shocks. Only this time the pen had low partitions over which the dogs could easily escape. The researchers presumed that this is what the dogs would do. But in this trial, when the dogs were shocked, they didn't even try to get out. They just lay down and whimpered. (Heartbreaking!) The researchers were baffled. The dogs had begun to exhibit symptoms resembling chronic depression. They learned from their first *horrific* experience that they were powerless. Then, when faced with the old familiar pain (the shock), even though the situation had changed (they could now easily escape the pen), they didn't even try to solve the problem. They generalized their conditioned experience of the earlier trauma to the similar (but different) situation—a situation where they could in fact escape what was causing them pain.

(This disturbing piece of research does at least have a somewhat redemptive ending: Martin Seligman went on to be a pioneer in the field of positive psychology, and today is a leading activist in the campaign to end cruelty to animals in the name of psychological experimentation.)

The moral? If you believe you're powerless to influence a painful situation, it makes perfect sense that you wouldn't waste your energy trying to change it. Instead, the obvious, logical response is to redirect that energy toward soothing your pain—curling up on the couch and licking your wounds. The problem is, if you've experienced learned helplessness, you're much more likely to believe that you do not have the power to change a painful situation, *even when you do*. But, thankfully, that is something you *can* change.

If you currently use food to soothe, you can learn the skills of solution-oriented thinking and task-oriented coping. These skills not only eliminate the need for Licking Your Wounds, they will have a profound impact on eliminating depression. I used to struggle significantly with depressed thinking, and of all the changes that I have made in my life in my journey toward freedom with food, changing from a powerless perspective to an empowered paradigm has rendered my life almost unrecognizable. This shift offers great relief for people who not only emotionally eat, but for those who engage in that painful style of depressed thinking and relating to the world. Learning the skills to replace learned helplessness—with an empowered, solution-seeking mindset allows you to eliminate and resolve the factors that cause you stress, directly. Without the assistance of cheesecake.

Just as the Mean Girl Munchies are characterized by quick, rapid-fire bites of crunchy foods, Licking Your Wounds tends to have its own defining characteristics. This eating is a much slower-paced, more indulgent and nurturing kind of experience. It is often done on the couch under a soft fuzzy blanket and the menu usually includes starchy, sweet, creamy foods, like ice cream, donuts, cupcakes, and frosting.

5. Recreational Eating

You're bored—and there's nothing on TV. Or you have a major project due. That you're anxiously putting off. Welcome to the perils of the fifth type of Non-Hunger Eating: Recreational Eating. You don't know what you want—but you're sure it's somewhere in your kitchen. So you start cupboard surfing. The next thing you know, you're standing in front of the fridge or pantry eating countless, random items. From various containers, and locations. You couldn't even say exactly how you got there.

Research on drug, alcohol, and food challenges shows that the number one predictor of relapse is the balance between obligation and pleasure in a person's life—the *Have To's* and the *Want To's*. People whose lives were more evenly split between fun things they genuinely wanted to do, and tasks that were hassles to perform, were far less likely to relapse. They were more successful in changing their undesired behavior. Of course, this makes perfect sense. If your day is one long, brutal grind, and the only thing you have to look forward to at the end of it are the Pop-Tarts and pizza that await you, it is only natural that you'd head home and eat through the rest of your night.

This type of Non-Hunger Eating is particularly evident during times of transition—when you get home from work, for example, or after you get the baby to sleep. You're tired. You've been pouring yourself out, giving your time to others all day. You want something for *you*—only you're too exhausted to figure out what that is exactly. And food is the easy go-to. The solution to this type of Non-Hunger Eating involves sprinkling activities that you genuinely can't wait to do throughout your day, week, and year. Giving yourself permission to include these things, and seeing the value of balancing pleasure and pursuit is key. The benefit isn't just a smaller skirt size—you'll actually end up creating a life that you can't wait to wake up to each morning.

IT'S NOT JUST ABOUT FOOD: THESE APPLY TO ALL RESTRICTED BEHAVIORS

These concepts don't just apply to eating. This is an important realization, because it can help alleviate that nagging fear that there is something wrong with you—that you are addicted to food, or broken. (*Which is not the case.*) Since these are psychological rather than physical reactions, they apply to any behavior you try to change via restriction.

While I was developing this method, I'd talk about my discoveries with my best friend—who just happens to be a naturally thin size zero. Chocolate didn't call to her—but purses, clothes, and shoes *did*. The same pain I experienced around food, she experienced around shopping. She didn't have thirty extra pounds on her body, but she did have thirty thousand dollars of debt on her credit card. She would often put herself on spending "starvation diets," only to end up Gasping for BCBG party dresses. Then she'd be left feeling so guilty for blowing her budget that she'd Shop Cuz She Shopped. Like is frequently seen with eating—she shopped when she felt powerless, stressed, or bored. And when she overdid it with shopping, then she shopped more, figuring—*What the heck! I'm already over my head in debt anyway.*

She was blown away as I described the five types of Non-Hunger Eating—because every single one of them applied to her struggles with spending. She was able to successfully use my method to regain a sense of control and mastery with her previously out-of-control spending. She successfully applied my principles to eliminate Non-Hunger Eating to her beyond-means spending. And, just as I would remind myself that there would always be more cupcakes the next time I got hungry—she assured herself that there would always be taupe patent leather Christian Louboutins the next time she got paid.

One of my brilliant clients, a stylish college student from Brazil, brought to my attention an excerpt from Martin Lindstrom's *Brandwashed*—a book that looks into how marketers manipulate our minds, and persuade us to buy. In the book Lindstrom writes about going on a brand fast for a year, resolutely depriving himself of brand-name products. At first, he expressed that not shopping was a welcome relief. But soon, he found that the more he deprived himself, the more products appealed to him. He reported even mundane items becoming "oddly alluring." Things like packages of mouthwash began calling to him from the supermarket aisles. Six months into his brand crash-diet, as he travelled to Cyprus to give a keynote presentation, his airline lost his luggage. Due to this unfortunate turn of events, he allowed himself to purchase one t-shirt, so he would have something to wear. And that single lapse spun out of control into a binge. He began Gasping for brands. Of this experience, he wrote:

[N]ow that I'd given myself permission to end my brand fast, the dam had burst. I went a little nuts. From then on I was buying San Pellegrino water, Wrigley's gum, and minibar M&M's by the caseload. Then there was the black Cole Haan winter jacket I bought in New York, and... the list goes on. Over the next few months I couldn't stop. You could have sold me roadkill, so long as it had a label and a logo on it.

So, the next time you're tempted to see your out-of-control

eating as a sign that you're broken, weak, or addicted—think of Lindstrom bingeing on brands. You are perfectly fine. (And normal.) It's your *approach*—dieting—that needs the overhaul!

LEAPS, STRIDES, STUMBLES, AND FACE-PLANTS— THE FUNDAMENTAL COMPONENTS OF CHANGE

Diets tell you what to eat and what to avoid. They never tell you *how* to actually go about psychologically making these changes in your life. Changing how you relate to food is about just that— change. There are ways to approach behavioral change that greatly increase the speed and ease with which you will succeed. There are also approaches (like beating yourself up for mistakes) that make failure a shoe-in. So let's take a quick look at the mindset that will catapult you toward success.

It is vital to be confident that you *will* succeed in your journey toward complete freedom with food and natural slimness— but to be *equally certain* that you will have significant, difficult stumbles along the way. You might be thinking, "Wait, that doesn't sound very positive!" But, in fact—*it is.* **Research shows that people are more successful in reaching their goals when they couple optimistic goal-attaining confidence with realistic expectations of a bumpy path along the way.** NYU psychologist Gabriele Oettingen found that women who had confidence that they would meet their weight loss goal lost *twenty-six pounds more* than those who doubted the likelihood of their success. (Nice!) But she also found that women who imagined they would have an *easy* time resisting the temptation to overeat lost *twenty-four pounds less* than those who anticipated they would hit bumps on their thinness journey and occasionally overeat—or at least really, really want to. She highlights the difference between the impact of expecting to succeed and the consequence of overestimating how easy or smooth the process will be. So, the optimal psychological mindset for successful goal achievement is to be a realistic optimist. Know that you will *absolutely* obtain your naturally lean body, but at the same time proactively (and realistically) assess the obstacles that you will face. This way you'll spare yourself the unnecessary anguish of misinterpreting inevitable challenges as signs of failure. (Never fun!) Instead, you can refocus all that energy towards outlining strategies to adeptly navigate those obstacles when they *do* arise. (Well, that and planning your new wardrobe.)

Have you ever tried something new in your weight loss efforts that worked really well at first? And you felt elated and free, like "this is it!"—only to slip up a few days later and end up thoroughly discouraged and tempted to ditch the strategy altogether? One powerful way to inoculate yourself from debilitating discouragement is to realize *from the beginning* that you will have times where you "slip up" and eat differently than you'd like. You don't go from Point A (the old behavior) to Point B (the new and improved behavior) in a perfectly ordered, neat and tidy fashion. **It is vital when learning a new skill—or unlearning an old one like dieting and Non-Hunger Eating—that you remember this: Change is not linear.** Somehow we expect that we'll learn the steps to the solution then promptly execute them, *flawlessly*. No! Behavioral change looks a lot more like a toddler learning to walk.

NAVIGATING SLIP UPS

Did you take your first step as a child, then promptly ditch crawling forever and enter your first 5K weeks later? Did you make it straight through to your third birthday fall-free without a single band-aided knee? I'm guessing—*not*. When you learned to walk, your first major achievement was likely the small act of grabbing the edge of the coffee table and pulling yourself up to a standing position. Woo hoo! And then—*crash*!! You fall back down. The next time you pull yourself up, you stand for a few seconds. Amazing! And then—*crash*, back down on your diaper-padded bum. This likely transpired over days, if not weeks, until one day you let go of the table and took a real, unassisted step. Victory! And then, you guessed it. *Crash!* You fell down again. Your gradual advances were coupled with setbacks, moving forward and learning more each time, until eventually… you're effortlessly running across a grassy field chasing a butterfly.

But can you imagine if the very first time that you fell after pulling yourself up on that coffee table, a voice came thundering down at you, berating you for falling? *"I knew you couldn't do it! You fell, you idiot! I can't believe you fell. Everyone else is walking, but not you. You are a pathetic little crawler and you always will be!"* No, quite the opposite! Toddlers are met with lavish praise at each minor progression, even steps in the general direction of progress. When the little one pulls herself up, she gets applause. Mom grabs the video camera and calls the grandparents. Can you imagine how different—*and by different, I mean better*—this journey would be if with every advancement you made, every small, wobbly step you took in the direction toward Hunger Directed Eating (however imperfect it was), you lavished praise, delighted wonderment, and encouragement upon yourself?

Rather than berating yourself for eating a little past full, you'd say, "Well, I used to plow *way* beyond full and not even really recognize that I was doing it, and today I only went a *little* beyond full. That is amazing progress! Way to go!" If you treated yourself this way, can you imagine the positive impact it would have on your continued slimming success?

The process of lasting change is messy. Most of the time you *will* be making great strides in the direction you want, but those bursts of learning and advancement will frequently be followed by slipping back a few steps. When you're tempted to beat yourself up for these normal (educational) missteps, think of the toddler learning to walk. If the child wobbled off balance and fell after a successful couple of days of walking, would you attack her with the venomous words you're about to unleash on yourself? Not in a million years! No, if it was a minor fall you'd probably give her a warm smile and make a fun acknowledging comment like "Oopsie" and laugh together about it as you encouraged her back to her feet. If it was a bad fall, you'd drop everything and rush to clutch her up into your tender, soothing arms, cradling her with soft, loving words as you gently tended to her pain. I invite you to experiment with responding to your own slips in this encouraging, supportive, productive way—the results will likely blow your mind.

MAKING PEACE WITH FOOD

Okay. So we've now seen that there is no such thing as a fattening food and that your metabolism is not an obstacle to your lasting leanness. We've also identified the *real* problem: Non-Hunger Eating. Which is simply starting to eat when you're not physically hungry and/or eating beyond being comfortably satisfied.

And we've examined each of the five types of Non-Hunger Eating: Gasping for Food, Eating Cuz You Ate, Mean Girl Munchies, Licking Your Wounds, and Recreational Eating.

Now, we're ready to explore, resolve, and eliminate the first type of Non-Hunger Eating, Gasping for Food.

chapter three

SO, YOU'RE REALLY NOT GOING TO TELL ME WHAT TO EAT?

Intro to Hunger Directed Eating

RECONNECTING WITH YOUR THIN-TELLIGENCE

So, Hunger Directed Eating (HDE)—what is this ingenious solution that brings bingeing to a halt? It is simply reconnecting with your innate thin-telligence: your body's signals of hunger, appetite, and satisfaction. The good news is, you don't even have to learn anything new to eat this way. This is exactly how you ate *before* dieting and emotional eating entered the scene. Responding to hunger and satiety is something that's already deeply ingrained within you. Look at an infant who can't walk, or talk—or even roll over on her side for that matter—yet she readily and perfectly responds to her internal signals of hunger and satisfaction. She cries for milk when she's hungry, then moments later firmly refuses the very same fluid when she's had enough.

I'll be teaching you *how* to get back in touch with your body's natural, built-in, weight-regulating system of hunger, appetite, and satiety. Physical hunger is the network of physiological cues signaling your body needs more fuel. Appetite directs you to the exact foods your body requires. And satiety indicates your body has obtained enough fuel, for now. These biorhythmic cues are designed to gently guide what, when, and how much you eat—from the inside out. Eating in response to this innate (and brilliant!) system equips you to easily obtain, and maintain, your naturally thin body weight.

THE FIVE STEPS OF HUNGER DIRECTED EATING

Hunger Directed Eating is made up of five practices that work together to put your eating—and leanness—on autopilot. With the right skills, your naturally thin eating once again becomes "set-it-and-forget-it," just like when you were a child. (If you've been arm wrestling with diets to lose weight, you'll likely need to see this one to believe it.) In the next five chapters we will be taking an in-depth look at each of these steps, along with skills that will equip you to implement them with ease. But first, let's take a quick look at each of the steps, and answer some initial questions you might have about Hunger Directed Eating.

Step 1: Eat when you feel physically hungry.

How do you currently decide when to eat? When you smell popcorn wafting from the office microwave? When you get home from work? When your show goes to commercial? You're about to swap these kinds of external eating triggers for your body's built-in slimming system. I'll show you how to easily recognize and respond to your true hunger signals. You'll soon become a pro at telling the difference between stomach hunger, which is real physiological hunger, and head hunger, which is that hankering to eat for *other* reasons.

Step 2: Eat what you really, really want.

So, you're physically hungry—now comes the fun part. No longer will you have to suffer pangs of "order-envy" from looking longingly across the restaurant table at your naturally thin friends' *real* food. Now you'll get to eat what you *really* want, too! First we'll dismantle your *incredibly understandable* fears of allowing yourself to eat the foods that currently torment you. Then, you'll master the trick of pinpointing exactly *what* your body wants and needs for optimal vitality, satisfaction, and svelteness.

Step 3: Sit down, be present, and thoroughly enjoy what you're eating.

We've all been there—numbing out in front of the fridge or TV, shoveling food into our mouths by the handful, straight out of the container or bag. We scarcely even realized *that* we were eating, let alone actually tasting and enjoying *what* we were eating. In this step you'll learn the small, incredibly doable tweaks that automatically slow you down and pop you back into the present moment, so you can savor and extract every last bit of pleasure from each of your eating experiences. Which is vital, because it is infinitely easier to stop eating when you actually feel satisfied.

Step 4: Stop eating when you feel comfortably satisfied.

Okay, this may sound far easier said than done at this point. But you'll discover the two keys that make it a relative cinch to push *any* food away once you start feeling full. Without willpower. Even a juicy burger, or a big hunk of rich, chocolaty, frosted cake.

Step 5: Check in. Notice how the food makes you feel.

Are you so "in your head" about what you last ate—feeling relieved if it was a salad, and guilt-ridden if it wasn't—that you forget to check in and see how the food makes your body feel? Step 5 will equip you with the quick-and-easy method to find out what your *body* has to say about what you last ate. Armed with this feedback, you'll be able to fine-tune—from the inside out—which foods work for you based on how they actually make you feel, and perform, in your day-to-day life.

Then, you simply wash, rinse and repeat all five steps as needed.

THE ELEPHANT IN THE LIVING ROOM: THESE ARE LEARNABLE SKILLS

Before we go on, let me first address the elephant that's glaring at us in the living room. It's not lost on me that if you sometimes feel out of control with food, being invited to "Wait until you're hungry before you eat" or "Stop when you feel comfortably satisfied," can feel as daunting and insurmountable as deciding to train for a marathon and then finding out that the first workout is a quick little 26.2 mile jog. It's like, *really? Obviously if I could easily wait until I was hungry to eat, I wouldn't be reading this right now. I'd be out cat-walking poolside in a string bikini*!

At first glance, it might seem like these steps assume that waiting until you're hungry to eat, feeling safe eating what you really want, and stopping when you're satisfied are skills you should *already* have under your belt. Not the case. First, I will teach you specific hands-on strategies, and paint-by-number techniques that make each step accessible—and actually doable. Second, it is helpful to understand that each of the HDE Skills work together and build off of each other for success. Practicing any single step alone is sure to be a real challenge. But, when you implement them together, you create a platform at each point that springs you forward to expertly navigate the next one.

It's like riding a bike. There are four distinct skills: pedaling, steering, balance, and brakes. If you were to attempt pedaling without balancing or steering, riding a bike would be incredibly difficult and dangerous to master—if not completely disastrous. Just like riding a bike, in order to achieve the desired outcome of moving forward with ease, you practice each of the different skills in unison. The learning process is not sequential. You don't master steering then move on to practice braking. Each part of the process is vital for the smooth execution of the next. If you skip one step, it will likely cause a pileup. For instance, if you wait for a good, clear hunger signal, but respond to it with bland restrictive fare, it's going to take a Herculean effort to put the brakes on when your body has had enough fuel, because you won't be even remotely satisfied—making it *much* more difficult to push the food away.

Also like riding a bike, you're likely to be a little wobbly and awkward at first—heart racing as you start down the road, your fingers tightly gripping the handlebars, your focus shifting between your feet on the pedals and looking up to navigate the path before you. *Is this hunger? Do I really want sushi? Is now when I should stop?* Some steps may come naturally, while others may take a bit more practice and exploration. But, it is by practicing each step in conjunction with the other four that your old (learned) eating habits fall away, and you create the environment where Hunger Directed Eating just becomes second nature.

WHAT HUNGER DIRECTED EATING WILL DO FOR YOU

HDE is the solution for the Gasping for Food response that research shows time and again leads directly to binge eating. It will alleviate, and ultimately eliminate, all of the chaotic eating behaviors brought into your life by dieting. A great way to identify what those behaviors are is to think back to the Ancel Keys study. Remember the one with the men in the '40s on the "Semi-Starvation Diet"? Each of the symptoms that sprung up in those previously functional men's lives after the study began are the exact symptoms that Hunger Directed Eating will eliminate. They developed an intense obsession with food. They felt out of control, sneaking and hoarding it. They binged on huge amounts of food, beat themselves up for eating, and experienced a ravenous, bottomless pit of hunger that knew no satisfaction. Hunger Directed Eating resolves all of this.

THE FIVE INCREDIBLE BENEFITS
OF HUNGER DIRECTED EATING

Your body has a brilliant and innate slimming system. When you take back control of your eating by responding to your body's gentle hunger, appetite, and satiety signals, you basically win the portable-obsession-free-peace-and-mastery-eating-any-food-without-deprivation jackpot! Not only will it enable you to get and stay thin, it will completely revolutionize how you relate to food—so that the process will take on a legitimate feeling of ease. And soon, you will enjoy the mastery and peace of these five incredible benefits of Hunger Directed Eating.

1. You will get and stay naturally thin in any situation.

In addition to being completely ineffective, dieting isn't very portable. A simple lunch out requires a complete menu calorie guide, a carb calculator, and a leaky bottle of fat-free dressing in your purse. With HDE you'll be able to lose, and maintain, your naturally thin weight—in any situation. That means being able to easily handle meal choices while on vacation, in restaurants, on the go, in your real, actual, day-to-day life. You can eat absolutely any food—without a pocket carb calculator. You will no longer be gripped with that "Oh no, what am I going to be able to eat?" terror when friends invite you over for dinner. HDE returns you to the deeply rooted, innate ease of relating to food that you had when you were a child, before you started dieting. These skills reside inside of you, and therefore are *always* with you. You'll be able to get, and stay, thin eating whatever you want, just like all of your naturally thin friends.

2. You will eliminate food obsession.

If you've been dieting for a while now, chances are at any given point in time you will have no idea where your car keys are, but you can rattle off, with great accuracy, what you've had to eat, down to the very last breath mint—for the past three days. Imagine all you could do with that reclaimed head-space. Preoccupation with food is the direct result of dieting. Period. HDE stops food obsession dead in its tracks. Relying on your body's signals to guide your eating unshackles all the energy you currently spend agonizing over food—those endless hours lost planning what you will eat, obsessing over what you won't, and tortured by what you can't. You'll swap food-fixation with an oh-so-welcome indifference to food, putting it back in its natural place in your life. Where, when you're hungry, you'll think about it quite fondly. But outside of hunger, food won't really come onto your mental radar, unless you're grocery shopping or planning a dinner party.

3. You will be free from the grip of "kryptonite foods."

Like Superman, every dieter has her kryptonite. The one food that is your ultimate weakness. Despite your overall strength, it's the single thing that can take down an otherwise invulnerable hero. The mere thought of being home alone at night with this food makes you quake with fear. Mine was cake. Birthday cake. Cheesecake. Wedding cake. Cupcake. Cake. Cake. Cake. Everyone has at least one. What's yours? The third benefit to Hunger Directed Eating is that it will release, once and for all, that kryptonite-like hold certain foods have on you. You're going to be able to eat absolutely *any* food in moderation—everything from hot fudge sundaes to hamburgers. Though once you've neutralized these foods, you'll rarely want them if their composition (sugar, starch, fat) doesn't give you optimum fuel. (More about that in Step 5.) My office is now happily situated above a premier cupcakery, and I'm delighted to say that it has about as much pull as the shoe repair next door. With HDE you'll be able to eat these highly charged foods, if you want them, and stop when you're satisfied. Because their power vanishes the instant you relax into the certainty that you can have them again *whenever* you want them. They're not going anywhere.

This means you can now keep previously tempting food in your house. Do you nervously pawn off the leftovers from a dinner party on your guests, the extra birthday cake, or the rest of that spinach dip the neighbors brought? Because you dread that torturous tension that awaits you the minute they leave, and you're alone. You hear the door click behind them. The food starts calling your name. Relentlessly. Until you finally snap, give in, and devour the entire container standing right there over the sink. Not only will HDE enable you to keep scrumptious food in your house, you'll soon have one of those deliciously giddy moments of going through your cupboard and stumbling upon a half-full box of Entenmann's glazed donuts that have gone stale because you completely forgot they were there. I know that probably seems unfathomable right now, but it'll happen.

My First "Forgotten Food" Moment

I remember my first forgotten food moment. It was a fluffy white three-layer cake with creamy coconut frosting. I bought it with great excitement, carved out a large tantalizing corner square, and put the rest in the freezer. Three weeks later, while rummaging through the freezer looking for frozen blueberries, I stumbled across it—all frost-bitten and iced over. I had *completely* forgotten it was there. Now, if your history with food is anything like mine, you fully grasp the monumental significance of a moment like this. Prior to becoming a Hunger Directed Eater, I would *NEVER* have forgotten about that cake. Are you kidding me?! There is no conceivable way I *could have* forgotten about it. It would have been relentlessly calling my name. In those days cake not only knew my name, but I'm pretty sure it also had the last four digits of my social security number! I would have obsessed over that cake with unrelenting fervor until I either ate it or destroyed it with dish soap and shoved it down the garbage disposal. With Hunger Directed Eating you'll soon be able to breeze in and out of your kitchen—even when it's packed with delectable fare—because the old anxiety and urgency will be *gone*. You'll be able to relax, knowing that these foods will never again be off lim-its. You can have them anytime. And you, too, will experience the incandescent bliss of finding stale Oreos in your cupboard.

4. You will replace feeling out of control with a sense of food-mastery and confidence.

How's your current self-trust level with food? Does the mention of going to a baseball game grip you with fear of being confronted with nachos, hotdogs, and beer? Does a dinner invitation incite a nervous scouring of the restaurant's online menu—scouting out acceptable, low-cal options? Hunger Directed Eating replaces your old out-of-control food feelings with a sense of mastery and confidence in *any* eating situation. *Okay, that one always makes me want to take a moment of silence.*

If you have lived under the tyranny of that out-of-control urge to eat—which overpowers you seemingly out of nowhere, causing you to chuck your diet out the window—then you realize the significance of what I'm saying. You know what it's like to suddenly transform into some kind of heat-seeking missile, locked on your target: that defenseless box of Krispy Kreme donuts—that seemingly *nothing* in that moment could stop you from devouring. All of them.

Before learning these skills, it can feel like your own worst enemy is lurking inside of you. You never know when *it* will strike. Seemingly out of nowhere, the urge ambushes you. You get blindsided with the urgent, feverish, out-of-control desire to binge, and feel utterly at its mercy. Terrorized. It feels so fundamentally unsafe to live inside of yourself. It's like there are two parts of you constantly at war. One part is trying to take great care of you by "being good on your diet," because you really want to be thin. The other part, also trying to take great care of you, responds to your need for freedom, variety, pleasure, and *normal food*—and revolts against your diet by giving in and over-eating. A turbulent war is being waged inside of you.

Hunger Directed Eating will restore your sense of wholeness and safety as you learn to reconnect with your body's hunger cues. It is the win-win solution that responds to, and satisfies, previously warring needs. You'll be able to be thin, healthy, and feel great about your body and appearance—all while enjoying delicious, *real* food. You'll navigate your mealtimes with freedom and flexibility, able to eat whatever appeals to you. You'll get back that sense of power, command, and choice with your eating. You'll fully regain that sense of self-trust that you so painfully lost. It will once again feel safe to live inside of you. You'll soon sail through the buffet table choices without a flinch. Nonchalantly order from that take-out menu that used to leave you cowering. You'll be your own boss again, confidently assured—"I've got this." And it is the best feeling ever!

5. You'll be able to get and stay thin without deprivation.

Fitting into that little black dress without deprivation is nice, and makes the process much more enjoyable—but it is *vital*, because the research is conclusive that deprivation leads directly to bingeing. (Without getting to Pass Go, or collect $200!) A slimming solution that does *not* involve deprivation is essential, because with restriction comes rebound eating, which completely undermines your efforts. When deprivation *is* involved, not only do the pounds stay put, your feelings of powerlessness soar. So, an eating approach that completely eliminates deprivation is not only favorable, it is *crucial* to successfully achieving your long-term leanness.

HOW HUNGER DIRECTED EATING CREATES A NATURALLY THIN BODY

Let's break down the foundation that's supporting this whole naturally thin philosophy, and why it works. First off, naturally thin people are, in fact, naturally thin. In contrast, people who are skinny but are *also* hyper-aware of calorie counts, what they eat, and what they weigh—are *not* naturally thin. My aim is to enable you to transform back into a naturally thin person, not someone who gets or stays thin by depriving or chastising themselves (or by having to exert a disproportionate amount of energy toward it either). **This book's goal is to teach you the skills that**

naturally thin eaters don't even realize they use. Naturally thin eaters function in a way that keeps them lean—effortlessly. And they maintain this svelte weight while eating anything and *every-thing* they enjoy.

If you eat like a naturally thin eater, *you will become naturally thin.*

Q: What if my body isn't programmed to be lean?
A: Your body wants to be thin more than you do. I promise.

Constantly being at war is exhausting. Constantly being at war *with your own body* is debilitating. As the research has proven, if you have a history of chronic dieting it's pretty much statistically guaranteed that you've been repeatedly unsuccessful at obtaining lasting leanness. So it makes complete sense that you might start to wonder if maybe your body just isn't cut out to be thin. Perhaps you've started to entertain the idea that you might have fat genes that are keeping you from your skinny jeans. I understand where you're coming from, but—NO. Your body is not a sadistic bully holding its ground and stubbornly refusing to let the pounds budge. Just to spite you. (Really!) Your body actually *wants* to be lean. It functions better without excess fat taxing its systems. Leanness is your body's natural and preferred state. All vanity aside. Hunger Directed Eating rebuilds a dieter's often-shaky trust with her body, enabling the firsthand (experiential) assurance and immense comfort of realizing that your physiology is working *for* you—not against you.

Not only is your body designed to be lean—it has the chops to get (and keep) you that way. Without your conscious help. Diet-logic suggests that your body couldn't possibly function effectively without a nutrition book and your constant caloric monitoring. Yet without your guidance, your body routinely accomplishes extraordinary feats! Take a paper cut for example. Did you know that if your body didn't automatically do the correct things in response to it, there are numerous ways you could *drop dead* from a simple paper cut? If the blood vessels near the wound didn't constrict, and the platelets failed to accumulate, forming a clot, you would bleed to death... *from a paper cut!* Or, if the leukocytes didn't show up to kill the bacteria, an infection could do you in. Or, if the fibroblasts got lost on their way to the cut opening, you wouldn't produce connective tissue, and the wound would never close. Without your body's genius systems in place, cutting your finger on an envelope could be fatal. Did you know any of this? I'm guessing, probably not. (I didn't either.) Yet, every time you've had a paper cut, your body reacted by doing *exactly* what needed to be done. Without your knowledge or assistance—you didn't even have to lift a finger.

In fact, in the time it takes you to read this sentence, your body has just produced 7.2 million new blood cells. It pumps out 2.4 million new ones every single second. Even when you're sleeping. Talk about an overachiever! And, again, all of this happens *without* your needing to intervene on the process. You don't need to know the function of a fibroblast for your cut to mend beautifully. You don't need to crack open a single physiology book for millions of blood cells to magically appear. Similarly, you don't need to know the carb count in a bowl of Grape-Nuts to get and stay thin—because your body has that covered. It uses the intricate systems of hunger, appetite, and satiety to take care of that for you.

NATURALLY THIN:
HOW YOU WILL BE LOSING WEIGHT

"So you're really saying that I can eat *anything* I want, and still lose weight?" If you think this prospect sounds too good to be true, I hear you. As I expressed earlier, it is both an important and empowering thing to understand all the facts when you're evaluating decisions that really impact your life. So let's look at the underpinnings of *why* this method works.

Beware of Focusing on Numbers

Before I get into this explanation, I want to make something very clear: I am *not* a proponent of focusing on or counting calories. *At all.* And even that is an extreme understatement. But to give you a better understanding of *why* naturally thin eaters are thin—and why eating this way will enable you to lose weight—I'm very briefly going to talk to you about how calories relate to the brass tacks of natural thinness. This is a simplified overview; we won't be getting into complex daily energy expenditure formulas.

Weight Loss Math

The only way to lose weight is to burn more fuel than you consume. Period. You can eat the healthiest *organic-low-carb-raw-vegan/vegetarian-gluten-free-Paleo* diet on the planet, but if you still take in more fuel than your body needs—you *won't* lose weight. In fact, no matter how nutritionally rich the food is you're eating, if you ingest more than is physically needed… you'll gain weight. Dieting makes so much sense on paper. You simply consume fewer calories by restricting what you eat, and theoretically you will achieve lasting leanness. However, there's a sticky *little* problem that gets overlooked within this seemingly straightforward calories-in-calories-out equation. **This purely academic formula for weight loss leaves out one vital factor: Deprivation leads to Gasping for Food.** Which (oh, right!) results in eating *more*—not less. And basically throws a big ol' monkey wrench into the works. Therefore, eating in a way that does not cause deprivation is equally as essential as consuming fewer calories overall.

The great news is—like automatically healing your paper cut—your calorie requirement calculations are handled by your internal biological systems. Without *you* needing to do any of the arithmetic. Your body's thin-telligence has that number balance covered. (Who knew your body was such a mathematical genius?) Hunger Directed Eating does not defy math, it simply uses your body's built-in programming to create the calorie deficit needed to obtain and maintain your naturally thin weight. *Without* deprivation. You eat what you want when you're hungry and stop when you're satisfied. Not only making your thinness sustainable, but effortless. Set it and forget it.

A Naturally Thin Example

OK, so let's say that your naturally thin friend generally eats X number of calories normally (without her awareness). She stays around 120 pounds without effort—and without actually *knowing* that she may weigh exactly 123.5 pounds at that precise moment. Then, she gets pregnant. She listens to her body's natural cues and gains the weight her body needs to create and sustain a new little human being. After she has her baby—as long as she doesn't disconnect from her body and diet to lose the weight—she will *naturally* make her way back to her lean starting weight, simply by listening to her hunger and fullness and instinctively following the guidelines I'm teaching you in this book. She isn't conscious of all these adjustments, her inborn system is taking care of it for her.

She never *unlearned* trusting her body.

Losing & Maintaining

Your body has an ideal naturally thin weight, even if you've never known (or experienced) it. When you start eating like a naturally thin eater—you will be eating the amount and types of food that you would at your effortless, joyful, peaceful, naturally thin weight. And because this is where you would *maintain* your naturally thin weight (like your 120-*ish* pound friend), you will *lose* weight until you reach this naturally lean version of your physical body. It is your personal, intrinsic (and amazing!) calories-in-calories-out balance. Who knew your body was so on your side, *right*?

So, to recap: It takes a certain number of calories to maintain a certain body weight. Naturally thin eaters respond to their hunger and fullness, instinctually eating the number of calories they need to stay at their lean weight (give or take a few pounds). When you learn and implement the skills and tools that naturally thin eaters use, you will ultimately eliminate the vast majority of Non-Hunger Eating calories you are now taking in. As a result of "reconnecting" with your body, you'll be eating within your naturally thin calorie balance—and will *lose weight* until you reach this lean version of your body. At which point this same amount of fuel will naturally keep you at your newfound thin shape, allowing you to effortlessly maintain your (lasting) svelteness just like all your naturally thin friends.

THIS IS NOT THE EAT-WHEN-YOU'RE-HUNGRY-AND-STOP-WHEN-YOU'RE-FULL DIET

It is *very* common to inadvertently turn Hunger Directed Eating into the Eat-When-You're-Hungry-and-Stop-When-You're-Full Diet. This completely undermines the effectiveness of these body-connecting habits by turning them into a diet with two rules—waiting until you're hungry and stopping the instant you're full. As we've seen, all sorts of things go (*terribly*) wrong when we introduce rules into our eating. Foremost, it leads directly to *more* overeating. When you eat a little past full it triggers your old diet-rule-breaking Mean Girl response and you can be very tempted to beat yourself up. *"I can't believe you didn't stop when you were full. You're never going to do this right! You're never going to lose weight!"* This pushes you right into the Mean Girl Munchies... and it becomes a destructive downward spiral.

When you find yourself Non-Hunger Eating and start feeling that anxious urgency to ensure it won't keep happening, that's when the idea of making "the plan" (to "undo" the damage) gets *very* tempting. But in reality, this "plan" will just reintroduce restriction that will result in another (likely bigger) Gasping for Food episode. Instead, the best thing you can do is to see what you can learn from that less-than-ideal experience. You will gain the most ground by extracting *actionable* information from the overeating event. Then, you can use what you learned to *prevent* it from happening next time. First, clearly identify what you did in the past in a similar situation when it felt easy to bypass the Non-Hunger Eating. What did you do that really worked? Then, isolate what was unique about this current (less successful) situation. There are two really helpful questions to ask yourself after a Non-Hunger Eating episode. The first is, "Was I feeling deprived in any way?" If the answer is yes, get really clear about how you created the sense of scarcity. Were you secretly avoiding carbs? Were you tracking calories in your head? You can then make sure to choose a more abundant approach in the future to bypass a deprivation-induced binge. The second question is, "What did I want the food to be or do for me?" Once you pinpoint *exactly* what you wanted those Ho Ho's to *do* or *be* in that moment, you have valuable information that can equip you to leap over that same obstacle next time.

OK, now that we have that out of the way—ready to start reconnecting to your naturally thin self?

chapter four

ARE YOU HUNGRY?

How to Identify Real Hunger and Avoid the
Counterfeit Calls to Eat

STEP 1: EAT WHEN YOU FEEL PHYSICALLY HUNGRY

Think about the last time you ate. What made you decide it was time? Did the clock strike twelve? Did your stomach growl? Did you hit a wall on a project at work? Step 1 answers the question, "When do I eat?" The answer being quite simply, when you're physically hungry. This chapter will teach you *how* to replace the external cues that used to signal it was time to eat—like the time on the clock or the smell of fresh yeasty bread as you pass a bakery—with your body's own built-in signals of physical hunger.

HELP! I'M TERRIFIED TO LET MYSELF GET HUNGRY! RESOLVING THE TWO COMMON "HUNGER FEARS"

Does the mere thought of physical hunger send your heart racing? If so, you are *not* alone. Whenever I present this idea of waiting for authentic hunger, whether one-on-one with a client or to larger audiences, I notice that people start to fidget in their seats. Variations of the same two very common concerns pop up—from Santa Monica to Sydney, Australia. After all, diet-logic has drilled it into you for years that you should go to great lengths to *avoid getting hungry*—as if hunger is dangerous and to be avoided at all costs. We'll soon be exploring the ins and outs of true hunger, but before we do, let's expose the misconceptions that tend to fuel these two "Hunger Fears."

1. But if I get hungry, I'll binge. Confusing hunger with the urge to binge.

It's *perfectly* understandable that you'd feel a little panicky about getting hungry if you're confusing physical hunger with Gasping for Food—that horrific, overpowering, almost savage drive to eat. This fear is fueled by the mistaken belief that hunger makes you vulnerable to the powerful (and painful) compulsion to binge. You can calm those concerns by remembering that it is *scientifically proven* that dieting (and a lack of certain coping skills) triggers binge eating—NOT physical hunger. If physical hunger were the impetus for bingeing, every infant, toddler, and naturally thin person would binge the instant their fuel tank dipped. The out-of-control urge to eat is not physical hunger at all, rather it is the powerful, and very real, Gasping for Food response that dieting creates—the *very thing* HDE eliminates.

That being said, it's very likely that being physically hungry probably *has* been strongly associated with the onset of a binge in the past. But, I'm going to go out on a pretty sturdy limb here and guess that hunger only ricocheted into overeating *after* you started dieting. Thus, activating the Gasping for Food response. HDE will enable you to eat like you did when you were a child. When you get physically hungry, you'll skip to the table and happily eat—and then get on with the rest of your exciting day.

2. Won't it hurt? Physical hunger is about as painful as the urge to blink.

Dieting can leave you anxiously cringing at the prospect of hunger, like a terror-stricken child waiting to get a shot. You're scared it's going to hurt! But in reality, physical hunger is *not* painful. Hunger is about as painful as the need to blink. Hunger is one of your body's perfect systems that expertly keep you thriving, healthy, and balanced. Your body sends gentle signals. Think about how your body indicates that you're tired. Really think about it. What does that sensation feel like inside of you? Do your thoughts move a little slower? Do your eyelids feel relaxed and heavy? Is there a warmth that comes over you? Our biological systems rely on *subtle* cues—like when your lungs need a little more air with a nice deep breath, or when your eyes seek more moisture with a soft, quick little blink. These promptings feel nothing like the fierce, out-of-control, Gasping for Food response. They are quite gentle, subtle, and soft.

If, however, you ignore any of these gentle cues, the signals increase in intensity. Have you ever held your breath for a long period of time? You start to feel dizzy. Your face gets red. You could even pass out. Think of the last time you bypassed your body's quiet call for sleep. When you haven't slept enough for a few days in a row, that feeling of tranquil, snuggly tiredness grows much more severe—and unpleasant. You're irritable. You're easily confused. Your vision gets blurry. Sleep experiments show that people can even have full-blown hallucinations from lack of sleep. In fact, sleep deprivation is officially recognized and regulated as a form of torture. (New mothers out there can attest to that!) Your body only sends loud (painful) signals to get your attention when you've ignored its initial, more polite requests. The urgent, loud, Gasping for Food drive to binge isn't physical hunger at all—it is your body shouting that restricting isn't working for you.

HOW TO IDENTIFY PHYSICAL HUNGER

So, if physical hunger doesn't hurt, what *does* it feel like? Once you're confident that it is safe to get hungry, the next feat is learning to recognize your body's voice in a crowd. There's a good chance that if you've been taught to fear hunger, or have confused it with Gasping for Food, you might not even really remember what true physical hunger feels like—let alone how to distinguish it from counterfeit calls to eat.

Physical hunger is gentle and energizing

Physical hunger is a gentle, hollow, warm sensation in your stomach, which is that fist-sized space right above your belly button.

So, if you make a fist and you place the bottom of it, where your pinky is, right above your belly button, the area covered by your hand is roughly where your stomach is located. Physical hunger actually feels great. You have a flood of energy when you're waiting for it to arrive. Digestion is a demanding process that uses a lot of your body's resources—being full really slows you down and leaves you sluggish. Whereas when hunger approaches, you feel really light, active, and energized. Hunger is a polite, quiet sensation. Just like all your body's other signals.

Physical hunger comes on slowly

Physical hunger comes on slowly. This gradual onset is a powerful key to distinguishing it from counterfeit hunger. True hunger doesn't unpredictably pounce on you, accelerating from 0 to 10 in seconds. No, physical hunger builds gradually. Your senses grow increasingly sensitive to food cues. You catch a whiff of the neighbor barbequing over the fence and you feel a pleasant, noticeable zing of interest. There is no urgency, just a calm prompting and heightened interest to make your way to food.

Physical hunger is sometimes accompanied by a warm gurgle, or growl, higher up in your stomach. Not to be confused with rumbling *below* your navel, which is most likely your last meal surfing through the later stages of your digestive process.

Physical hunger is flexible and open to options

When you're physically hungry, you're open to options. You'll tend to gravitate toward broad categories of food: something substantial, or something savory. True hunger is more flexible, and easier to satisfy than pseudo hunger. It is open to suggestions. Real hunger is *not* that laser-focused hankering for a specific food—*I must have the fresh breadsticks with cream cheese artichoke dip from "such and such" restaurant.*

Physical hunger is accompanied by a heightened sense of smell and taste

To this day, I will never forget a dinner party I threw *years* back. I was doing my best to serve dinner at the designated time, but due to a brief kitchen blaze the meal was, uh… significantly delayed. (Don't ask!) When we *finally* sat down to eat, I apologized for making everyone wait. In response to this, one of my naturally thin guests sagaciously replied, in his posh British accent, "Hunger is the best seasoning." And it completely blew my mind—it is *so* true!

One inherent perk of HDE is that your sensory pleasure experience for each meal is cranked up to its absolute apex, simply by waiting until you're truly hungry to eat. Physical sensitivity to food cues is dramatically heightened when you're hungry. You get what I call "the bionic nose." You can smell bread baking three miles down the road. This is great, because it's not only the smell that is intensified. The *flavor* is amplified as well. Food tastes its absolute best at the *exact* time your body actually needs it. (Talk about win-win!)

Physical hunger lacks indecision

One (huge) standalone trait of physical hunger is that you aren't riddled with indecision or uncertainty about eating. When your body is truly hungry—you know it. You don't second-guess.

Uh-oh, am I hungry? Should I eat? No, it is quite clear. *I'm hungry. Get me to food.*

Putting it all together: Physical Hunger

Gentle polite feeling + Heightened taste + No indecision = Physical Hunger. What could be better? Sign me up, *right?*

HOW TO IDENTIFY COUNTERFEIT HUNGER

What craving sucker punches you the very instant you step foot inside a movie theater? Popcorn, right? At the mall? Cinnabon. After a grueling day at work? Anything, and *everything* in the fridge. Counterfeit hunger is the cleverly disguised urge to eat—for reasons *other* than physical hunger. Fake hunger is a learned response to emotional distress, diet restriction, and conditioned cues. Like popcorn at the movie theater, you've been conditioned to want it. Some call it emotional hunger or head hunger. It's that nagging, urgent drive to eat that is completely independent of your body's need for necessary nourishment. Counterfeit hunger is fueled by habit, like always eating when you watch TV, or a desire to soothe emotional discomfort. The ability to quickly distinguish real hunger from fake hunger will save you oceans of grief. So, let's take a closer look at the telltale signs of this counterfeit hankering to eat.

Counterfeit hunger comes on suddenly

Pseudo hunger is characterized by a *very* sudden onset. It goes from 0 to 10 almost instantly and is highly susceptible to the power of suggestion. You're walking through the airport, you smell the intoxicating aroma of butter and fresh-baked dough, and suddenly you *must* have a gourmet soft pretzel. Or you see gooey cheese stretching from a slice of pizza during a commercial break and instantly you're famished, and what a *coincidence*, totally in the mood for pizza!

Counterfeit hunger is tied to emotional distress

Counterfeit hunger tends to spring up during tough emotionally charged moments—but in a bind, any emotional moment will do. You're nervous. Mmm, potato chips. You're bored. Pretzels. You're lonely, or feeling stuck. A chocolate snack cake two-pack. In addition to emotional junctures, transition times between one activity and the next tend to be another frequent fake-hunger hangout. You've just gotten home from a taxing day at work and aren't quite sure how to unwind. Bam! All you can think about is food. If you're upset and the pull to eat is *not* accompanied by the physiological hunger indications outlined above, chances are high that what you are feeling is *not* the real deal.

Here's a good question to help rule out fake hunger in those moments: "If I were feeling cheerful and had something incredibly exciting to do right now, would I still want to eat?"

Counterfeit hunger is never satisfied

You're bored. There's nothing good on TV. You start foraging the cupboards for something to eat, but you're not quite sure what you're searching for. So, you munch on some baked chips. No, that wasn't it. *Hmm, maybe chocolate chips?* You graze on a few handfuls of those. *No. Ooh, what about the leftover pasta in the fridge?* A few fork swirls later... *Nope.* Despite your copious sampling, you can't seem to find anything that will satisfy your hunger. **Not being able to reach satisfaction is a powerful indicator you are not operating in the realm of physical hunger.** Another variation on this theme is when you eat massive amounts of food—enormous cartons of steamed rice and orange chicken (that could easily serve a family of four)—yet you don't feel satisfied. That "bottomless pit" sensation is a sure sign that you've temporarily disconnected from true hunger and fullness.

Counterfeit hunger is marked with urgency, guilt, and indecision

Another tip-off that you're dealing with fraudulent hunger is that it is accompanied by urgency, guilt, and indecision. Your head spins with a cacophony of food-chatter. You feel nervous about making the "right" decision. It is a thankless state—you're tortured by cravings, and then racked with guilt when you eat.

Putting it all together: Counterfeit Hunger

Fake hunger is a ghastly combo-platter of negative feelings! Wild urgent desire to eat + Highly specific cravings + Indecision = Counterfeit Hunger.

PHYSICAL HUNGER OVERVIEW

So, quick review. Physical hunger is a quiet, gentle feeling sometimes accompanied by a hollow, warm sensation in your stomach—it feels great, and you feel energized while it's building. While counterfeit hunger is the sudden, nagging, often wild, urgent, insatiable desire to eat. This usually indicates that there is something else going on, and you're likely using food to change how you're feeling, or to rebound from restriction.

THE HUNGER SCALE

One helpful tool you can use as you're getting back in touch with your body's hunger signals is the hunger scale. It is a tool to rate your hunger from One to Five:

One: you're full, you don't even want to *think* about food.

Two: you're pleasantly satisfied; you stopped at the right place and you're done.

Three: you're feeling neutral; you're not hungry, you're not full. It's that perfect, balanced place.

Four: you're feeling pleasantly hungry; this is a great place to start eating. You're really interested in food, you're starting to feel light and empty, you feel hollowness in your stomach—you're ready to eat.

Five: you've bypassed your initial hunger signals and you are feeling *extremely* hungry.

Most people find it enjoyable to move within Two and Four—between pleasantly satisfied, and pleasantly hungry.

One way to play around with this tool is to arbitrarily check in several times a day, and see where you're at on the scale. This gives you excellent practice at rating your hunger and satisfaction. So, right now, where are you? Are you a One? Are you full and can't even think about food? Two, pleasantly satisfied? Are you Three? You're good, you're not hungry, you're not full. Are you at Four? You're pleasantly hungry; you might even be heading right now to go get something to eat. Or, are you Five? You're extremely hungry and just about to put a bookmark in this page because you *must eat*.

HOW OFTEN WILL I GET HUNGRY?

The time between hungers is determined by two factors: the composition and quantity of the food you last ate, and your body's fuel efficiency (i.e., your metabolism).

What You Last Ate

If your last meal was a porterhouse steak with a sour-cream-packed baked potato and two dinner rolls slathered in butter—then it's going to take hours longer for your body to signal hunger again than if you ate, say, a small bowl of vegetable soup. The type and amount of food you eat will determine how long you remain sustained. Certain foods take longer than others to digest because of their composition. A cucumber is mostly water, so it is going to fly through your system *much* faster than a cheeseburger. Additionally, different nutrient properties have varying effects on your blood sugar. As a general rule, foods that cause your blood sugar to spike—simple carbohydrates and refined sugars—will trigger an abundant release of insulin, which lowers your blood sugar. The insulin-induced sugar crash will leave you feeling hungry, often ferociously so, really soon after you eat. (We'll talk about sugar-crash hunger more in Step 5.) That's why on those mornings you eat your body weight in pancakes with syrup, you are left ravenously craving sugar just forty-five minutes later.

Your Fuel Efficiency (Metabolism)

The second factor that determines how soon you'll feel hungry after a meal is the rate at which your body uses up fuel—its gas mileage. So, if you're moving around a lot, revving your metabolism, you'll get hungry more quickly than someone who spends the hours after her meal reading and relaxing on a beach chair by the pool.

Hunger is not a slave to the clock.

Hunger is not a train. It doesn't abide by a schedule. Just because it's "dinner time" doesn't mean that your body needs fuel. However, once you start responding to your true hunger signals, the erratic Gasping for Food eating relaxes, and your hungers will start to take on more comfortably predictable patterns.

You can ditch "Preventative Eating."

Eating now because you *might* get hungry later is like pulling the fire alarm now because the candles might set the drapes ablaze… next Tuesday. "Preventative eating" is a common dieting practice. This is the post-dated eating you do when you're leaving the house, and you're not hungry. But, since *they* say that you're not supposed to let yourself get too hungry, you figure—I better just eat now *in case* I get hungry later—in a well-intentioned attempt to inoculate yourself against (dreaded) physical hunger. Hear this: **It is impossible to satisfy a future hunger.** If you're not physically hungry and you eat, your body doesn't need the fuel, so it stores it for later—on your thighs.

If dieting has bashed you about in a push-pull relation-ship with food, it probably feels incredibly frightening to carry snacks around with you. You dread the battle. The relentless chatter—*Don't eat it!* EAT IT! *Don't eat it!!* EAT IT!! *Argh!!!* Pure torture. But, as your eating begins to normalize, now you'll actually be able stash food in your purse or desk so it's available when you *are* hungry—and feel nothing but sweet relief at that prospect.

What if I'm hungry and I can't get to food?

The only thing more terrifying for a former dieter than being alone in a room full of food is being hungry in a room *without any* food. So, what happens if you're hungry and you can't get to food? Well, in that case, your body's going to sig-nal hunger and when it doesn't get an answer, it will ring back in about 15 minutes with another wave of signals. If you're not able to grab a meal, your body will simply pull from your reserves (a.k.a. your belly and thighs) and convert that stored fat into fuel to get the energy it needs. But again, the goal is *not* to skip meals or bypass hunger as a means to lose weight. Routinely ignoring true hunger backfires by triggering Gasp-ing for Food—which ultimately undermines your leanness goal. So, while it is perfectly normal to put hunger on hold every now and again when your schedule is bustling, it is *not* an effective shortcut to skinny.

As for physical sensations, if you ignore your body's hunger signals and don't eat, you may get a slight headache or feel a lit-tle grumpy. And if you let it go on too long, you will feel light-headed, weak or dizzy. But again, that's only if you put off eating for a *significant* period of time.

BETWEEN HUNGERS

It's far easier to hear someone calling your name when you're in a quiet room than it is when you're in a boisterous crowd. So, at first you might want to allow for a really clear, authentic hunger signal. To do this, I encourage you to skip sugared drinks, or coffee with milk and sugar *between* your hungers, so that it won't play games with your blood sugar and interfere with your true hunger signal. This is just in the beginning as you're learning to recognize your hunger signs. So, if you're drinking anything other than water between your hungers, I recommend you have something unsweetened or possibly sweetened with a natural sugar alternative like stevia.

On a (purely scientific) side note, the *Yale Journal of Biology and Medicine* reports that artificial sweeteners "encourage sugar craving and sugar dependence"—which ironically defeats the whole purpose, don't you think? So, health consequences aside, you may want to start noticing whether artificial sweeteners are impacting your cravings. If you *do* find them fueling a sugar-mania, you can always take the (brave) plunge to explore natural sugar substitutes.

What if I'm still not sure if I'm hungry?

Well, a very reliable gauge is, if you're not sure, chances are you are *not* really physically hungry. That doesn't in any way mean to then restrict and turn this into a rule—the eat-when-you're-hungry-stop-when-you're-full diet—and say, "I can't eat now." If you're really, really wanting to eat, allow yourself to sit down and enjoy some of what you're wanting. I know that diet-logic tells you to white-knuckle through these situations. But, the *last* thing you want to do is build up restrictive tension by skipping a single cookie, and inadvertently set yourself up to gasp for the entire bag.

REMINDER: THIS IS NOT THE "WAIT-TILL-YOU'RE-HUNGRY" DIET

It can be *very* tempting to unintentionally turn "waiting for hunger" into a diet rule. This is completely normal, especially if you are transitioning from years of rules-based eating. When you find yourself getting "rules-y" about waiting for hunger, remind yourself that rules are what got you into this mess in the first place. By keeping "waiting for hunger" in the *general-guideline-of-things-that-make-you-feel-good* category—like resting when you're tired—you accelerate your speed of mastering this skill and landing at your naturally thin goal.

So now that you know how to recognize a loud, clean, physical hunger signal you're ready for the best part—deciding what you want to eat.

chapter five

WAIT, I CAN REALLY EAT ANYTHING I WANT?

How to Get and Stay Thin Eating
What You Really, Really Want

STEP 2: EAT WHAT YOU REALLY, REALLY WANT

We've made our way to the most exciting part of the entire Hunger Directed Eating process—and the most terrifying—eating what you really, *really* want. It's *exciting* because now you can eat anything you want: bread, pasta, pastries, Mexican food. Anything. And it's terrifying because *now you can eat anything you want*: French bread, pesto fettuccine, apple strudel, cheese-stuffed quesadillas. There is no food list for Hunger Directed Eating—because your body doesn't need one in order to (expertly) achieve your natural leanness. But if there were a HDE food list, just think of its sheer magnitude, it would contain every single food that exists. Talk about creating a feeling of abundance!

Once you've established that you are in fact physically hungry, Step 2 addresses the question "What can I eat?" The answer being—quite refreshingly—absolutely *anything* you want.

Previously you've always outsourced this decision to your diet plan. When it came time to eat, you'd consult a list of incredibly enticing foods—those in the forbidden category. Then, you'd look at a *far* less enticing list of foods—those in the permitted category. And you'd make your selection based on the confines of those parameters. Totally easy, *right*? *(Not!)* It's 7 o'clock at night, you've had a long, hard day at work, and you only have half a protein and a serving of fruit left on your food exchange list. But what you really, *really* want is a big piece of deep-dish pizza. But that is not allowed. So you settle. You forsake what you really want for the promise (and fading hope) of being thin. Which, if it actually worked might be an acceptable trade-off—but the *maddening* part is, even when you were suffering through not eating what you really wanted, you *still* weren't losing weight (or keeping it off over the long run).

The goal of Step 2 is to reconnect with your authentic appetite. Plugging back into what you really want when you're hungry will guide you to making the most physically, psychologically—and emotionally—satisfying food choices. Eating what you genuinely desire sets you up for slimness success in several ways. Especially when it comes to the often-intimidating step of stopping when you've had enough fuel. It is *infinitely easier* to stop eating when you feel physically and mentally satisfied with your meal. And your chances of feeling satisfied are maximized when you eat what you really, really want—rather than what you think you *should*.

Let's take a look at the benefits of eating what you want, the common concerns that pop up around this step, and the nuts and bolts of *how* you actually go about doing it.

THE BENEFITS OF EATING WHAT YOU REALLY WANT

Chances are you'd rather walk a tight rope than be alone in a room with an entire pan of warm, fudgy brownies. Eating what you really want is *by far* the most terrifying step for former dieters. More than all of the other four steps *combined*. So, if eating what you want is so scary—why do it? What's in it for you? Great question. There are three powerful advantages to eating what you really, really want.

1. It Stops Gasping for Food in its Tracks

How much do you think Eve would have really wanted that apple if she lived on a twenty-acre apple orchard? Surrounded by barrels brimming with Fujis and Pippins—with *full* permission to eat them. Apples on demand. Now, if within this apple grove a single avocado tree suddenly emerged, from which she was expressly forbidden to eat—can you venture to guess her new kryptonite obsession? Garden-evicting guacamole, anyone? A food only has magical magnetic powers over you if it is forbidden. (Or if it's in limited supply.) By giving yourself permission to eat any food, you cut the Gasping response off from its source. Diet-induced overeating is caused, maintained, and fueled by *one* thing—deprivation. By forbidding certain enticing foods, you've inadvertently kept a steady stream of deprivation fueling the powerful pull toward them. Which has kept their kryptonite powers alive and thriving.

Removing the floodgates from their hinges

At any given time, it's likely you're only ever in one of two states of being—you're either on a diet or breaking your diet. You ride the pendulum between these two painful extremes—ricocheting between dieting and bingeing, restricting and overeating, being "good" and giving in. You tell yourself you can't have it, which only makes you want the restricted food all the more. Back and forth you go. *I shouldn't. But I want it. I shouldn't. But it looks so good, and I had such a hard day!* Until finally the battle gets so intense that you cave. You let yourself eat it. But it doesn't stop there. Oh no. Then the Gasping kicks in, because you know that the floodgates are going to close soon—and there is no knowing when you're going to allow yourself to eat that desired, *delicious* food again. So, you eat as much as you can while the gates are temporarily open. Makes perfect sense.

By legalizing all foods, you are sending the message loud and clear: Restriction is *over*. From now on, the floodgates will remain permanently open. In fact, they have been removed from their hinges. These foods will never again be forbidden. As you begin to truly trust that you won't pull the rug out from under yourself by restricting certain foods again, you'll notice your eating start to relax. The constricting grip of the Gasping response will soften, and ultimately release. Because it's been cut off from its life source—deprivation. You'll be able to confidently enjoy these previously off-limits, highly charged foods in beautifully moderate portions. By allowing yourself uninterrupted access to them, the power certain foods once had over you will fade away. Formerly banned foods will become neutral. *Like any other food.* When you're hungry and in the mood for it, it's very appealing—but otherwise it's pretty uninteresting. You'll notice it becomes really easy to stop eating halfway through *any* of these foods. You'll feel able to peacefully push the rest aside when you start feeling satisfied, because you'll be certain, and truly trust, that the food isn't going anywhere. The next time that you want this particular item, it's going to be there—and more importantly, you're going to let yourself have it.

2. It Makes it Easier to Stop Eating

Do you currently get blindsided with grief three-quarters of the way through your meal, when you realize that soon you'll have to say goodbye to the food and end the enticing eating experience? Eating what you really want maximizes your satisfaction, which makes it much, much easier to stop eating. You'll be able to actually register when you've had what you need, because your preferred food choice will truly satisfy your hunger—both mentally and physically. Physical satisfaction isn't the only factor that influences satiation; psychological satisfaction plays a key role in the process as well. If you wanted something savory and substantial like a turkey burger with grilled onion and avocado, no amount of steamed broccoli is going to give you the sense of satisfaction required for you to effortlessly push the remaining food away.

Let's look at the alternative. What happens when you *don't* allow yourself to eat what you truly want? I'm guessing that you may be familiar with this drill. While having coffee with your friend earlier in the day, she offered you half of her gourmet peanut butter cookie, which looked utterly delectable with its huge milk chocolate chunks and actual pieces of peanuts. And even though you *really* wanted it, you turned it down. Because sweets are a no-no and you were being "good." And now, *hours later*, that cookie is still on your mind. So, you go to the fridge and munch on a handful of baby carrots. But they don't really do the trick. You nibble on a couple Saltines. No, that's not doing it either. Maybe you need something sweet? You've got it! You dab some jelly on the Saltines. Negative. Hmm, maybe a handful of cereal? You bury your hand in the box. Nope, *still* not it. Fast-forward thirty minutes, and you're in the mini-mart parking lot anxiously polishing off an entire box of (second-rate) cookies in a hurried, frantic manner—with a bag of chips and a king-size Twix standing by on deck. All because you turned down that amazing cookie. You could have spared yourself those 3,000 extra calories, and bypassed immeasurable pain and remorse (not to mention enjoyed infinitely more satisfaction), if you had just let yourself eat the blasted 200-calorie half a cookie three hours ago—when you really *wanted* it.

3. It Eliminates Food Stereotype Overeating

We often turn to external (almost moralistic) groupings of food, fully anticipating that these distinctions will guide us to eat less "junk food" and more "healthy" fare. The logic seems reasonable. Sadly however, research shows that classifying foods as "good" and "bad," or "healthy" and "fattening" sets you up for an overeating train-wreck—overindulging in the "healthy" foods *and* bingeing on the "junk food." (For those of you keeping score at home, that's a resounding lose-lose.)

Stereotyping chocolate as "fattening" and cottage cheese as "healthy" makes you eat more of *both* categories. There are two cognitive distortions that contribute to this kind of behavior. First, by classifying a food as healthy, people erroneously believe that consuming even large quantities of the "good for you" foods won't negatively impact their weight. Calories are calories. If you eat more than your body needs—no matter how righteous the food— your body will *still* store the excess on your stomach and thighs.

Research bears this out. Food stereotypes were examined in a study where subjects were asked to rate what was more fattening: a single miniature Snickers (not the Halloween fun size, the *tiny* square one in the gold wrapper), or a bowl of cottage cheese with pears and carrots. Time and again the dieters rated the Snickers as more fattening. But in reality, the mini Snickers was only 47 calories, while the cottage cheese option weighed in at 569 big ones. Food classification results in a belief that if a food is "healthy" it's harmless to consume—even in large amounts. Remember the diet-logic mantra from the fat-free craze of the '90s? "If it's fat free you can eat the whole bag!"(Yet, startlingly still feel *far less* satisfied than with one "real" cookie.) This misconception can definitely be hazardous to your waistline.

The second problem with food stereotyping is that when people label a snack as "fattening," they believe that eating even a *small* amount will promote weight gain. While Eating Cuz You Ate might not be the most logical food behavior, there are actually a few different dieting circumstances that incite it. We already know that exceeding your pre-allotted calories in a sitting is a powerful trigger to throw in the towel and continue to overeat. But another, far more insidious, instigator is eating something from an off-limits food category—even in a *very* small amount. Participants believed that even a *very* small amount of a "bad" food would promote weight gain, and was therefore enough to trip the "What the heck, I've already blown it, I may as well keep on eating" response. This is how a dieter can have a single 35-calorie bite of a candy bar explode into a 3,000-calorie binge. So, by ditching food stereotypes, you spare yourself from the inclination to overeat "healthy" food and "junk" food alike.

THE TOP 3 FEARS ABOUT EATING WHAT YOU REALLY WANT

The giddy excitement of being able to order anything you want off the menu is likely to come with a fair number of concerns. This is perfectly normal. If you've experienced the pain of being very out of control with food in the past, suddenly allowing yourself to eat whatever you want can be terrifying—*deeply* terrifying. The especially unnerving part is that, because of how deprivation works, the foods you've felt the most out of control with (and subsequently forbade yourself to have) are the very ones you'll probably want the *most* at first. So, let's shine a light on each of these fears to ensure that you feel really safe while using this approach.

Fear #1: If I let myself have whatever I want, all I'll eat is junk food.

"Wait a minute Josie, if I let myself eat whatever it is I want, I'll end up eating nothing but chocolate cake and tater tots." Well, here's the thing, you probably will—at first—if that's what you restricted. It's a scientifically documented phenomenon that people gravitate toward a forbidden food once it is reintroduced. A study examining the impact of restriction on food preference divided children into three groups. The first group was not allowed to have sugar, candy, or sweets. The second group was forbidden fruit. They could eat whatever else they wanted, but fruit was off-limits. And the third group had no restrictions. When the constraint period was over, the children were invited to eat from a buffet with a large assortment of foods. The children with no dietary restrictions sampled a variety of the foods. Those who were denied sugar rushed to the candy, while those who had gone without fruit made the same rapid beeline toward the strawberries and cantaloupe. So yes, at the beginning it's very likely you'll strongly gravitate toward whatever you restricted. If you restricted sweets and carbohydrates, you'll probably want candy, muffins, and French bread. If you restricted high-fat food, chances are you're going to be drawn in that direction. Having a heightened desire for what had previously been prohibited is the natural human response to deprivation. Allowing yourself uninterrupted access to the particular food (when you're hungry) and noticing how that food makes you feel (energy, satiation, mood) are the most expedient ways to rid high-tension foods of their power.

How to Re-Introduce Kryptonite Foods

When introducing kryptonite foods back into your life, it is very important to do it in the way that best supports you. There are no hard-and-fast rules. One size does not fit all. The entire message behind this approach is to listen to your gut (literally and figuratively). Me? Personally, I went all out. When I started this process many years ago, I cleared out an entire shelf in my cupboard, even going as far as lining it with fresh drawer paper. I took a breathless trip to the grocery store and loaded up my cart with every food item I'd ever wanted, but had forbidden. And I do mean *everything*. Ice cream. Entenmann's. Pop-Tarts. Doritos. Nutella. Fettuccine. Chili lime tortilla chips. I even went as far as to buy an entire sheet cake with colorful buttercream frosting balloons emblazoned with the words "Happy Birthday." I went BIG.

But just because full immersion works well for some, doesn't mean it will be right for you. A more gradual approach has proved successful for many of my clients who found themselves emotionally eating the "fun foods" once they were in their house. They saw a tremendous decrease in their binge eating overall, so they knew that giving themselves uninterrupted access was the answer—but while they were adjusting, they benefited from doing it in a way that reduced the probability of emotionally eating.

They were able to harmoniously satisfy their need for freedom with food and safety from overeating with the modified approach. First, they let themselves order what they wanted when they were out. If they were craving Chocolate Blackout cake, they'd go to the high-end bakery up the street, order a piece, and enjoy it with a cup of coffee. This was a double-win as it kept the food out of the house *and* had them in public while they were eating. Several clients reported that eating in public supported a feeling of being present while eating the high-tension food, and made them feel more "civilized" than they might if they were home alone. Or say… in their car. Once they quickly mastered the kryptonite foods in public, they would begin to bring single servings into the house. They'd buy a brownie, or a single-serving bag of chips, and only have a day's supply in the house at a time. One of my clients in South America, was thrilled to find individual-serving packets of Nutella. This way if they had an emotional eating hiccup, or nervousness about a food—that exaggerated its pull—there was a much smaller total amount of that particular food calling them to consume it. Finally, once they mastered bringing those smaller amounts of the foods into the house, they graduated to larger portions: a full-size carton of ice cream, a whole bag of chips, an entire box of cookies. This systematic, incremental approach afforded them the ultimate win-win of releasing the brake while still creating a safe environment until their food chatter fully faded away.

Fear #2: If I eat fattening foods, I'll gain weight.

The second fear that usually springs up is, "Wait a minute! If I'm eating all this fattening food, I'm going to gain weight! That's the *last* thing in the world that I want!" But as we saw in Chapter 2, there is no such thing as a fattening food, and it is mathematically impossible for caloric density to make you gain weight. When you're eating within the confines of hunger and satisfaction it doesn't matter, from a caloric balance perspective, if you are eating a spinach salad or a super burrito. Let's say that your body needs 500 calories of fuel. When you're hungry, even if you choose what you *really* want, your body will register when you've eaten enough of the desired food to reach that threshold. Your brain will send signals of fullness after two-thirds of the spinach salad with apples and blue cheese, or after a third of the mammoth burrito. But it's essential that you're eating what you want, so that you'll be *psychologically satisfied* by the time your body sends you the signals that it's had enough. When you are eating what you want—starting when you are hungry and stopping when you are full—weight gain is *not* part of the equation.

Fear #3: Eating this way can't be healthy.

The third concern that grips people is, "There is no way it can be healthy for me to let myself eat what I really want." It's common to think that when dieting you eat healthier than when you're just eating "free-style." Research makes it clear however, that although they start out with good intentions—dieters' healthful eating is swiftly undermined. Dieters alternate between periods of successful restraint and periods of extreme indulgence. Remember the milkshake study? You start out juicing and making salads, and by the end of the week you're doing a nosedive into a platter of deep-fried mozzarella sticks with a side of ranch.

Hunger Directed Eating *will* result in your consistently eating healthier than you have ever imagined possible—however, the vehicle that gets you there is highly counterintuitive at first glance. I realize that this flies in the face of just about everything you've ever read about how to lose weight. But if nutritional knowledge and resolutions truly enabled you to consistently eat healthful foods, we likely wouldn't be having this conversation right now. Right? Of course it's completely natural to worry about your health if you think you're going to be eating a diet that's filled with chips, and burgers, and pastries. But here's the thing—*you aren't going to be drawn to those foods for long.* This very process is what enables you to *consistently* eat healthful foods (that are custom tuned for your body). Because letting yourself eat what you truly want eradicates the psychological pull toward certain foods. Foods that currently drive your best weight loss intentions off the road, and into a ditch.

With that kryptonite pull of restricted foods finally out of the way, for the first time, you'll be in a place where you are choosing what you eat—*it* isn't choosing *you*. You'll be able to nurture and fuel your body with an inside-out approach to nutrition, by listening to what it really needs. And you'll be amazed by all your body teaches you along the way. In Chapter 9 I'll tell you how within months of eating this way I cured a skin rash I had for over *20 years*—that stumped doctor after doctor, after doctor (who *all* wanted to put me on steroids!). By finally quieting my food chatter, I was able to listen to my body's aversion to a specific food, which turned out to be the *cause* of the rash all those years.

I very rarely crave any of the foods that I ate during the early stages of Hunger Directed Eating, and now I mostly eat foods that powerfully fuel my body. I truly *desire* them. Don't get me wrong, I eat something sweet just about every single day, but now a square of chocolate or two peanut butter chocolate malt balls is all I usually want. There's no willpower, no resolution, just pure authentic desire for very nutritious foods. And it was only possible to get to this place through the Valley of Donuts and Doritos. Because it was there that I silenced (*once and for all*) the chatter and the pull of that rebound eating which consistently tripped up my nutritional best efforts.

The exciting news is that you absolutely *can* lose weight during the initial stages of this process—even when the food pull is still quite strong. As you reconnect with your body's thin-telligence you'll likely move through three phases. Let's take a look at the journey to the land of Pure Hunger Directed Eating.

THE THREE PHASES OF HUNGER DIRECTED EATING

Phase 1: Donuts and Doritos

After years of low-cal *this* and low-carb *that,* you finally get to eat the real thing. Phase 1 is the honeymoon period where the brakes are released and you'll likely find yourself wanting the "fun foods" that have been banned. However, this in *no way* means that you won't lose weight during this phase. In fact, most people lose considerable amounts of weight in the Donuts and Doritos phase. I personally dropped several dress sizes in this early stage, eating cheesecake and chips daily. I rarely desire those foods now, but it was essential that I let myself have them, and is exactly *why* I seldom want them today. Recently I instinctually (and in hindsight rather impolitely) curled my lip up when offered Nutella by a friend. And let me tell you, Nutella and a spoon were my *Holy Grail* during Phase 1. But now, years later, the thought of it is *genuinely* unappealing.

Releasing the Brake–A Shortcut Through Donuts and Doritos

The trick to expediting the trip from Phase 1 to Phase 2 is to completely release the brake, and really allow yourself to consume your desired, previously forbidden, foods. This uninterrupted access ejects those foods from their current elevated, pedestal place and brings them back down into the realm of common, normal food—stripped of their magical, magnetic power that used to pull you towards them.

Geneen Roth, the celebrated author of *Women Food and God* (and one of the warmest, *most present* women I've ever had the pleasure to meet) tells of when she first released the brakes on her eating. She had a lot of chatter, cravings, and nervousness around cookie dough. So, she gave herself full permission to eat cookie dough *anytime* she was hungry. Picture this process: You're going about your day, and you get hungry. So, you go into the kitchen, pull out the flour, butter, brown sugar, eggs, and rich *real* chocolate chips—and whip up a little bowl of cookie dough heaven. Not to bake. Just to eat. Which, let's admit, is *pretty exciting*. You then grab a spoon, sit down at the table with a napkin and a glass of ice water with lemon, and start to eat it. At first, it's going to be a smooth, sweet explosion of deliciousness in your mouth as you chew the creamy dough punctuated by bits of crunchy, rich, chocolaty chips. Pure bliss. Initially, it might actually be a little hard to put the spoon down and stop eating when you've had enough, but you do. A few hours later you get hungry again. You pop into the kitchen, whip out the bowl of cookie dough, sit down, and carve out a few more bites. That evening when hunger approaches (you guessed it), you mosey up to the table with your faithful bowl of dough.

But, the next morning when you wake up and you start to feel hunger, the golden glow surrounding that cookie batter is going to start to fade. It will soon drastically lose its appeal. What used to be a heightened, bewitching, contraband treat suddenly plunges from its all-powerful position—to a beige blob of blah. You'll start craving something light and crisp and watery, like a nice, tart, juicy green apple with unprecedented fervency. Your body's thin-telligence is designed to motivate you to seek out a variety of foods to ensure you'll get the spectrum of nutrients it requires. But when we stick our nose in, interfering by making certain foods off-limits and other foods "shoulds," we throw the entire system out of whack. We foul-up this perfectly well-functioning process and start Gasping for

Food, overriding our physiological appetite with an exaggerated (psychological) gravitation toward whatever is deprived.

A few summers back, one of my best girlfriends took her three daughters to a weeklong day camp, where she was an instructor. These were *really* long days. They would get up early, go to the camp, and not return home until well after the summer sunset. So, as you can imagine, a week like this was filled with on-the-go foods. They were having hot dogs with packets of chips during that day at camp, and take-out pizza or drive-thru tacos on the way home at night. Finally, the end of the camp came, and my girlfriend wanted to treat her girls for being such cooperative angels through such a grueling week. "Hey guys, tonight you can have anything you want for dinner," she offered from the front seat. "What will it be?" And in a chorus of emphatic voices the three girls responded, "Mommy, can we *please* have salad?" And now, whenever one of our lives get really hectic, we always jokingly ask, "Is it a kids-craving-salad kind of week?"

Phase 2: Combo Platter Eating

The second phase is a mix between pure Hunger Directed Eating and Donuts and Doritos. You're listening to your body, but there is still a bit of an exaggerated pull toward items previously banned from your menu.

Phase 3: Pure Hunger Directed Eating

The third phase is pure Hunger Directed Eating, where between eighty to ninety-seven percent of the time you're eating purely what your body desires for fuel. This is an important point to note. Somehow we have the misguided notion that naturally thin eaters *never* eat when they aren't hungry. Not so! In fact, it is really useful to study your naturally thin friends and identify when they *do* and *don't* eat beyond hunger. When they do overeat, it is usually around rare foods like their Aunt Dianne's ambrosia salad. Or at Thanksgiving, where most foods are rarely (if ever) consumed at any other time of the year, and it's uncertain when they will have access to them again. So you'll be comforted to know that when your naturally thin friends *do* overeat, it is from the very same cause, they are Gasping for foods that have been made *situationally* scarce.

FOOD PREFERENCES– DOES THIS WORK IF YOU'RE A VEGETARIAN?

But what about if I'm a vegetarian? What about religious food observances? Many people wonder if Hunger Directed Eating will allow them to eat according to their moral or religious preferences. The fascinating thing is that when an individual eliminates a food group for reasons of deep personal meaning, they are making that choice from the inside out and it does not trigger the Gasping response. It is a choice. Not a prohibition. And therefore does not create a feeling of deprivation. When eating choices come from deep value attachment (inside out), even in the height of binge eating an inside-out vegetarian isn't going to be out of control with sausage. If you want to honor certain food observances, the key to making them stick—just like each of these others steps—is to attach your choice to your internal values, *not rules, restrictions,* or *regulations* from the outside in.

HOW TO DO STEP 2:
EATING WHAT YOU REALLY WANT

So now that we've explored the benefits and concerns around letting yourself eat what you really want when you're hungry, let's focus on *how* you actually do it. It's actually very simple; there are just three steps.

1. Move all foods into the "No-Guilt" category

The first step is to make all foods legal, permissible, and *morally equivalent*. I always laugh when I hear women say, "Oh, I've been really good today." and they are in no way referencing spreading peace and joy through the world, or helping people in need. No—they mean that they had an egg white omelet instead of cinnamon French toast. So the first step is to move all foods into the "no guilt" category. Give yourself permission to eat any food. Let me insert a little medical disclaimer here: Consult your doctor first, as this guideline is in no way, shape, or form intended to replace any medical advice. So, if you are allergic to a food or your doctor says "no saturated fat," or "no high glycemic index foods," *listen to your doctor*.

Create Two New Food Categories

Previously you likely classified foods as "good" and "bad," "diet" and "fattening," or "healthy" and "unhealthy." Now, you'll only need two categories based on preference and performance. The first will simply be foods you *like* and foods you *don't like*. Easy enough. The second category is determined by how the food makes you feel. You will have foods that make you feel *great* and foods that make you feel *crummy.* So for me, cupcakes originally fell into the "like" and "make me feel crummy" categories. As I became more aware of how tired and grumpy I felt after eating them, they fell dramatically from their high preference standing. These two categories will evolve and influence each other as you gather feedback about how the foods you like make you feel—over time you'll gain a better (and more nuanced) understanding of what foods really work well for you.

Portia de Rossi was interviewed recently by *Marie Claire* magazine about how she healed from her painfully disordered and chronic restricting, and when asked about her current diet she replied, "I have a very, very healthy relationship with food, in that I eat whatever I want, whenever I want. I never restrict quantities or types of foods. Everything that I want, I allow myself to eat. As a consequence, I have a very kind of regular, normal diet, and it's not perfect. It has a kind of smattering of junk food in there. It's because I allow myself to eat potato chips if I want potato chips, and candy if I want candy. I never, ever restrict food, and I will never go on a diet ever again." And I say, hey, if it's good enough for Portia, it's good enough for me.

2. Keep a wide variety of foods available and accessible

The second step in setting yourself up to make the most satisfying food choices is to keep a wide variety of foods both *available* and *accessible.* There's an important distinction between these two.

Available

Keeping the foods you want *available* basically means keeping them on hand—in your fridge, in the cupboards, at the office. It's perfectly normal if reading the last line triggered a red alert concern, especially if in the past you have felt really out of control with food. Chances are there are certain foods that call to you if you keep them anywhere near you, and instigate a raging internal "Eat It," "Don't Eat It" tug of war. That is an intensely painful battle, and it makes complete sense you would want to avoid it at all costs. Those warring desires are the result of restricting. Remember, it is actually by making these foods available that you zap their magnetic powers. Like the modified option for re-introducing kryptonite foods, you can use the same approach while you are adjusting to making a variety of foods readily available. To relieve the concern of going overboard, simply keep smaller amounts of foods you really want on hand.

Keeping food available *and* out of sight

Out of sight, out of mind. Literally. One immensely supportive tip while you're transitioning into keeping desired foods available is to keep them visually out of sight. Have a separate cupboard and drawer in your refrigerator, where you store the more charged foods. This way, when you're going about your daily life, grabbing a glass of water in the kitchen, you don't see chocolate-covered almonds and get sucker-punched by the power of suggestion.

At first, it helps to visually obscure highly charged foods even *within* the cupboard. So, when you're making breakfast, or putting together your kids' lunches, you don't unexpectedly come face to face with one of your treasured treats while reaching for the canister of oatmeal, or grabbing a juice box. One trick is to put these foods in a cupboard that's away from your normal fare—like where you keep your kitchen mixer, or with other appliances you don't use very often. In the fridge you can keep them in a specially designated crisper drawer, so they're visually shut off.

The mere sight of food can trigger a strong signal to eat it, in two very powerful ways. The first is *psychological*: the very influential power of suggestion. You pass the receptionist's desk, and spy a colorful bowl of M&M's. *Suddenly* you *must* have M&M's. Visual suggestion is a strong behavioral trigger. It is the foundation of the billion-dollar marketing industry. Companies spend millions for a two-minute Super Bowl commercial, because they know how powerfully suggestion influences what you'll choose to do, and buy, and often—*consume*.

Food also fires off a strong *physiological* response. Researchers measured the insulin response in people who were presented with food, and found that visual exposure to food spiked people's insulin levels, which is associated with storing body fat. Participants also reported stronger cravings for the food they saw. So a casual glance at the breadbasket creates a biochemical response that makes you want to eat—*even if you're not hungry*. Who needs that? This is easily remedied by keeping all foods completely out of sight. You can stash particularly compelling foods in rarely visited drawers so you don't ignite the visual spark and trigger to desire them if you're making meals for others. This particular tool is very helpful when it comes to supporting yourself while making that very scary transition of bringing these foods into your home. Soon, when those foods are neutralized, it won't matter what you do with them. You could even keep a tower of donuts on the table in the entry hall and it *still* wouldn't call to you if you weren't hungry. But you would end up with A LOT of stale donuts.

Accessible

You're *famished*—and running behind. You've only got ten minutes to eat something before you have to fly back out the door. What you're really craving is fruit. You dash to the kitchen, but since you splurged on some exotic options last time you went shopping, you're confronted with either a giant pomegranate or a *whole* fresh pineapple. Delicious, yes, but *what* were you thinking? Even though you'd really prefer to have the fruit, you don't have the time to (safely) hack open the pineapple or to fish out the pomegranate seeds—well, not without ruining you new cream-colored cardigan. So, you fling open the cupboard, grab a handful of Hershey's Kisses, and you're off!

Foods are only available if they are actually *accessible*. As psychologist Signe Darpinian points out, it's important that you have a selection of foods equally accessible. When you're hungry and in a time crunch it helps to have a variety of foods that you can eat within the same amount of time. So cutting up the watermelon and boiling the eggs ahead of time will afford you the luxury to choose what you really want—even when you're in a rush.

3. Make the most satisfying food choice

Here comes the fun part. You've waited for hunger, you feel that gentle, hollow little nudge in your stomach. Now you get to figure out what you want. It is important to remember the fact that true satisfaction is multi-dimensional—with both physical and psychological factors. The best food choices will meet both of these, maximizing your ultimate satisfaction. There are two simple questions that help powerfully guide your selection.

THE TWO SATISFACTION-BOOSTING QUESTIONS

1. What do I want?

The first question is, (are you ready for it?) "What do I want to eat?" I know that sounds ridiculously simple like, "Duh, Josie!" But for those of us who have dieted for so long, it might have been *years* since, when faced with a food decision, you actually asked yourself what *you* wanted. There can be a lot of healing and beauty in this question. The decision of what to eat has been outsourced for so long—to a diet, or magazines, or the current trend of what you should and shouldn't eat—but now you get to take back that power. Look inside of yourself and ask, "What do *I* want to eat?"

You might know immediately what you want. But, if dieting has you a little out of practice, you may not have *any* idea how to narrow down your preference. So, here are some questions to help you hone in on what it is you actually want:

Heartiness: Do you want something really filling and substantial, or do you want something light?

Temperature: Do you want something warm? Or, are you more in the mood for something cool?

Texture: Do you want to spoon something creamy and smooth, or munch something a little more complex and crunchy?

Flavor: Are you in the mood for something sweet, savory, salty, sour? What flavor intensity are you desiring? Something really robust and flavorful, or do you want something a little more mellow or bland? These questions will help you pinpoint exactly what you want.

2. How will this food make me feel?

The second question that supports you in making the most satisfying food choice was something I learned from grilling my naturally thin best friend. She wasn't even aware that she habitually asked it. But after she graciously let me question her off and on for months—during which she constantly baffled me by doing things like taking three bites of cheesecake at a party—eventually, I was able to break down the process. When faced with a food decision, she'd first get a couple ideas in her head of what she wanted. Then, she would imagine how this food was going to feel in her body. Both right while she ate it, as well as how it was going to feel over the next few hours. This practice builds a feedback loop between Step 2 (what it is you want), and Step 5 (how the food actually makes you feel). Think of the times you've eaten something and were then saddled with sugar-induced mood swings or intestinal ice-picks for the hours following. This question builds an invaluable bridge between desire and the actual pleasure payoff. Which in time renders *how* the food makes you feel inseparable from whether you really *want* it. (Um. Priceless!)

WHAT HAPPENS IF I GET TOO HUNGRY?

You've been stuck in a class or meeting, and you're *starved*. Your blood sugar has taken a dive and is now hanging out in the shallow end of the pool. While heading home your brain rattles through the different options of what you could eat. Suddenly, you remember the frosting in the bottom left of the fridge door, and one thought starts looping: *Oh man, a couple big spoonfuls of frosting sounds so good right now.* It is really common to crave a quick sugar fix when your blood sugar has dipped. However, if you follow that up with the second question: "How is this going to feel in my body?"—then vividly imagine and play out the next few hours—it may alter your desire. Personally, if I were to eat a few spoonfuls of frosting, I know that within 30 minutes I'd feel exhausted, irritable and edgy, with a side of fuzzy brain. And after the crash, I would crave sugar by the truckload. So, once you play that scenario out, you're much more likely to think *Hmm, okay, the frosting does sound really good, but I'm not sure if I want to make the commitment to feel that poorly over the next few hours.* So, it will take you back to the drawing board. *All right, I'm wanting something sweet.* I've learned that when I'm wanting a treat and it's still in the middle of the day (where I don't want to have a crash like that) there are certain things I can eat that won't act like an anvil dragging down my afternoon energy. For example, if I have a piece of chocolate with nuts in it I feel fine. So, a square or two of chocolate or a couple sips of fruit juice will quickly pop my blood sugar back up high enough for me to sanely get to a real, satisfying meal.

Give yourself room to explore. You likely won't know at first how certain foods make you feel. The only reason I know how terrible pastries make me feel is that I ate them in beginning phases of Hunger Directed Eating. I would eat sweets in the middle of the day—when I was hungry—and noticed that my productivity would go into a tailspin in the hours that followed. I soon made the connection, and those foods swiftly lost all mid-day appeal. So rather than getting nervous and "rules-y," I invite you to approach this process with a curious, exploratory mindset. You're simply gathering data to assist you the next time you're hungry, so you can make a highly satisfying choice in a snap—from the inside out.

Now that you know how to recognize when you're physically hungry and how to pinpoint what you really, really want, you're ready to learn how to eat in the way that makes it a *cinch* to stop when you've had enough.

chapter six

FOOD BLACKOUTS & TRUE SATISFACTION

How Enjoying Your Food and Psychological Satiation will Make You Slim

STEP 3: SIT DOWN, BE PRESENT, AND THOROUGHLY ENJOY WHAT YOU'RE EATING

Have you ever been eating a sandwich while working at your computer, and as you're plugging away you reach for the second half of your sandwich, and your hand hits the empty plate? It's—gone. Yet, you have *absolutely* no recollection of eating the second half of that sandwich. In fact, if you weren't home alone you'd start interrogating others, accusing *them* of eating it. Step 3 of Hunger Directed Eating eradicates these common "food blackouts" by equipping you with the skills to sit down, be present, and really enjoy what you're eating—every time.

SATISFACTION MAKES YOU SLIM: THE ROLE OF PHYSICAL AND PSYCHOLOGICAL SATIATION

Thoroughly enjoying your meal is more than a simple pleasantry—it is absolutely imperative if you want to get and stay thin. Your body has two distinct systems that signal satiation. The first is the physiological network that sends *stomach-up* messages to your brain via blood sugar and stomach acid levels, indicating when your physical nourishment needs are met. **Physical satisfaction** is impacted by the amount, type, and characteristics (e.g., protein, fiber) of food you consume. But there's a *second*, often overlooked but equally essential, system housed in your ventral hypothalamus, which sends *brain-down* messages signifying **psychological satisfaction**. There are far more variables to how a food makes you feel than its simple nutritional breakdown. Eating environment, freedom of choice, and perceived portion size are just a few of the factors that contribute to and make up psychological satisfaction. The reason you care about either of these is that satisfaction—both physical and psychological—is the key that unlocks the secret of *how* to easily push food away when you've had enough.

MINDLESS EATING–THE SATISFACTION THIEF

Distraction is the enemy of satisfaction. Engaging in other activities while you're eating poses a serious threat to both physical and mental satisfaction. Splitting your focus between eating and other diversions, liking watching TV, runs interference with your ability to detect your body's subtle satiation signals—making it easy to plow right past full as the car chase heats up on your show. Consequently, it is much more difficult to read your body's polite message that it has obtained its fuel needs when you aren't attending to the eating process. Similarly, eating while multi-tasking erodes satisfaction, because the magazine, blog, or vexing conversation you're replaying in your head has your attention—not the food. So the first moment you actually realize you're eating pretzels—while trolling through Pinterest—is when your hand hits the salt on the bottom of the bag and they're already gone. (Bummer!) By that point it's too late to enjoy them.

You're about to learn the seven habits employed by the naturally thin that will automatically maximize the pleasure and contentment you derive from *each* of your eating experiences. You'll master the skills of satisfaction—making each meal so satiating that it's going to be cinch to stop eating when you've had enough. (Cue *Hallelujah Chorus!*) Plus, you'll learn how to adeptly navigate some of the "highly caloric" tricks our minds play on us around psychological satisfaction. In addition to maximizing satisfaction, and thus eating less, this step *powerfully eliminates* the two types of mindless eating.

Mindless Eating Type 1: Zoning Out

Does eating ever seem to hypnotize you into some kind of zoned-out trance? Your methodic hand-to-mouth movement and rhythmic munching soothes you as you completely check out. Zoning Out is a way of enabling your brain to take a break from all the stress in your life—allowing your senses to call a time-out on the constant stimuli that bombards you. Unfortunately, one of those things that you're fuzzing out is your body's signal that you've had enough to eat. This type of mindless eating occurs when you let your consciousness drift from your body and meal, causing you to temporarily disconnect from hunger and fullness.

Mindless Eating Type 2: Pavlovian Eating

The second type of mindless eating that's eliminated by Step 3 is Pavlovian Eating. These are the conditioned, learned responses where you crave certain foods as the result of environmental triggers that actually have *nothing* to do with physical hunger. You might be familiar with Ivan Pavlov and his dogs. He was a Russian scientist who won the Nobel Prize for his work around conditioned reflexes. Every time he fed his dogs, they would see the food and start salivating in anticipation of eating it—a normal response. He then rang a bell each time he brought the food. Bring the food, ring the bell, bring the food, ring the bell. After pairing these activities enough times, eventually he could just ring the bell and the dogs would begin to salivate, triggering their physiological anticipatory food response *without* a single of morsel of food in sight. This concept of an altered response occurring when two stimuli are repeatedly paired in close succession resulting in the response (salivating) originally given to the first stimulus (the food) being elicited by the second (the bell) is called Classical Conditioning. And it accounts for *thousands* of unconscious calories consumed in front of the computer and TV.

DISMANTLING YOUR FOOD BOMBS

We tend to have a minefield of food triggers sprinkled throughout our lives. Think about it. When you walk into a movie theater, what is the food that you instantly crave? Popcorn, right?

You probably don't go to the movies and suddenly have an over-whelming desire for a jelly donut. Why? Because time and time again going out to the movies has been paired with hot, buttery popcorn. Just like Pavlov's bell paired with the food, all you need to do is step one foot into the theater and ding! You want popcorn.

We're about to dismantle the landmine of conditioned eating triggers you may have inadvertently created by habitually pairing eating with various locations and activities. It's likely that currently, simply sitting in that certain spot on the couch, standing by the sink, or watching shows on your laptop, detonates a flurry of conditioned triggers fueling a strong desire to eat when you aren't even hungry. And who needs that? You're about to learn how to snip the tripwires that you may have set up in your home, car or office, that trigger you to eat—*independent* of being hungry.

THE SEVEN HABITS OF HIGHLY SATISFIED EATERS

Satisfied eaters do seven things you can use to maximize your pleasure and awareness while eating, making it a whole lot easier to stop eating when you've had your fill. These skills all fall under what I like to call the three S's: sit, silverware, and savor. Let's take a look at each of these Seven Habits of Highly Satisfied Eaters.

Habit #1: Give Yourself Permission to Eat

Okay, I understand that this may sound overly simple, but if you've been dieting for a while, chances are very high that you're living in such a chronic state of restriction that you never fully give yourself permission to eat. Instead, you eat with one foot in the meal and one foot out of the meal. I remember at one point in college having the startling realization that I *never* completely committed (or consented) to my eating experiences in an intentional way. And I definitely didn't allow freedom for my physical and emotional preferences when I ate. I was either eating under tight vice-grip restrictions or completely out of control. I was obsessed with food, but it had become so terrifying that I was nervous to actually enter into a meal. Restriction had so thoroughly eroded my sense of mastery with food that eating felt painful and dangerous—something I almost wished I could avoid altogether. But you've got to eat to live. And so, I lived with this. But you no longer have to settle for the constant tension-filled push-pull—you can release that by deliberately choosing to be "all in" when you eat. If you have a lot of painful ambivalence around food, the next time you're hungry I invite you take a moment before your meal and really give yourself *full* permission to eat.

Habit #2: Sit and Eat in Designated Eating Zones

Selecting predefined eating locations powerfully deactivates landmine food triggers, and completely turns the notion of "sneaking food" over on its ear. Somehow we think that if we're standing, or doing something else while we're eating, the calories don't count. The whole concept of sneaking food makes me laugh—*now*. I remember one pivotal moment when I was in the kitchen, hunched over, sneaking the last few cookies from the package. And I suddenly had this revelation, "Wait a minute, who in the world am I sneaking this from? *I* know I'm eating it. The people in the other room don't care if I'm eating it. And my hips and thighs *surely* know I'm eating it." It was definitely a breakthrough moment in my relationship with food.

(Saying this, I want to make it perfectly clear that I recognize that there can be situations where you may be eating in front of people who *are* in fact judging you. When you internalize their perceptions, it can be extremely hurtful and corrosive to your sense of self-worth. If the judgments of others are something that causes you consistent pain, I highly recommend that you consider reading any of the truly life-changing books by Marshall B. Rosenberg. He teaches how to eliminate suffering by understanding the true message behind the criticism of others.)

Where do you currently eat? Take a minute, even pull out a piece of paper and write down the five, or more, places where you currently do that majority of your eating. Is it standing up in the kitchen? In front of the open refrigerator? The driver's seat of your car? At your computer? On the couch in front of the TV? *Get really specific.* Do you sit on the right-hand side of the couch, or stand by the cupboard on the left, near the microwave in the kitchen? Is it at your desk at work? My guess is that you have several places where you do most of your eating. I'm also guessing that a significant portion of those places are areas where you do *other* things—like watch TV, read, or search the internet. As Pavlov illustrated, by pairing eating with areas where you do other important activities, you set yourself up to trigger the powerful urge to eat every single time that you're working at your computer, driving your car, or watching TV. And that adds up to a TON of additional Non-Hunger Eating.

You can completely eliminate these Pavlovian eating triggers by making a single adjustment: Create a Designated Eating Zone. This is the one place where you do all of your eating, and that place is to be used for *nothing else*. So it's a good idea to have that place be at a table. (Rocket science, right?!) If you have an eat-in kitchen and a formal dining room, of course it can be two places. But it is essential that it is a place where you eat and do not do *any other* activity. This way you free yourself up to extinguish and deactivate all those triggers scattered throughout your environment that spur you on to eat when you're not hungry.

One great side-benefit from using a Designated Eating Zone is that it begs the question each time that you're about to munch on something, "Am I really hungry? Am I willing to commit, and go sit down in my spot and eat this?" If not, the chances are you're eating out of habit, or maybe for some emotional reason, but it's not physical hunger. It's a fabulous little built-in hunger verification tool. At first, I sat in my Designated Zone for every single thing I ate—and it really helped. When I made cookies and I wanted some dough, I would spoon some into a ramekin and savor it in my designated spot. As Hunger Directed Eating becomes more natural, you will naturally grow more flexible, but at the beginning it is ideal to keep your eating in one to three selected eating spaces, where you don't do *anything* else.

Eating at Work

A Designated Eating Zone is even effective if you routinely eat at work. I was a database architect when I first developed these principles and I frequently ate lunch in the office. My desk was L-shaped and I did the majority of my work to one side where my main computer was located. When I decided to eat, I would make a clear break from work, launch my screensaver, turn to the left side of my desk where I never worked, and I would eat. And do nothing else. When I was satisfied, I'd stop eating, put the food away out of sight, then turn back to my original location and resume working. I realize this might sound a little extreme. But designating eating zones clearly delineates, this is where I work, and that is where I eat. Thus eradicating the trigger where firing up your computer suddenly makes you crave a white mocha with a vanilla bean scone.

Eating in the Car

Let's face it. We *all* eat in the car sometimes. Especially with how on-the-go life tends to be. As a general habit it's best not to eat in your car because the distractions of driving minimize satisfaction—and you end up with hot sauce on your cashmere cardigan. Oh, and um, that *other* little thing… eating kind of distracts from you from driving safely. But, every now and again eating in the car is going to happen. One of the beautiful aspects of this method is it allows flexibility; where, no, it's not a habit that you eat in the car, but if you're in a crunch, you absolutely can. If you *are* going to eat in your car, it is ideal to pull off the road (for numerous reasons). I was such a die-hard at the beginning of this process that if I was going to eat in the car, I'd pull over and sit in the passenger seat, to avoid a Pavlovian association between driving and eating. Nerd, I know. You don't have to go that full-bore unless you really want to, but at least pull over so you can (safely) maximize satisfaction and awareness of what you're eating, making it easier to toss the food when you're done.

Habit #3: Display Your Meal on a Plate

So, when you *are* hungry and you've given yourself full permission to eat, and have chosen your designated eating spot, you're ready to benefit from the third habit of Highly Satisfied Eaters. Which is to put your *entire* meal out in front of you—visually—on a plate. There are two reasons why this is really beneficial.

Eating with your eyes

We've all heard the saying "His eyes were bigger than his stomach." While this saying has some negative connotations, harnessing the power of your eyes' visual connection to your stomach (and satisfaction) can actually be a really *good* thing—especially when you make the following strategic tweaks to how you (literally) see your food. There are two major factors that contribute to psychological satisfaction. The first is selecting what you really want, but there's also a very significant visual component. Actually seeing your food—a nice substantial serving on a plate—sends the message of abundance to your brain. Visually absorbing your meal in front of you powerfully contributes to emotional satisfaction. When your brain registers an abundance of food and sends the message, "Okay, I've had enough. I'm satisfied," it's *much* easier to stop. Picture this. Say you are going to eat 24 bite-sized crackers, and you consume them by repeatedly burying your hand deep in the box, pulling out one or two of them, and then popping them into your mouth. You only ever see one or two crackers at a time. That is going to have a very different impact on your psychological sense of satisfaction than if you took out a bowl—especially a very small bowl—put the 24 crackers in it, and looked at them as you ate. From the beginning you'd see the large portion of crackers before you. And as you ate them, every bite would be mentally registering as part of the plentiful initial serving. This reinforces, from a psychological standpoint, that you're enjoying an abundance of food, contributing to your overall sense of satisfaction, and (*time for the broken record*) making it easier to stop.

Commit to what you're eating

We've all done the noncommittal food dance. You know, the one where you have mixed feelings about eating a piece of pie, so you go into the kitchen, get out a knife, and you shave off a paper-thin slice and eat it. Then you go in the other room and think, "Wow that was so good. I need another bite." So you go and nervously carve another itsy bitsy sliver. All the while thinking, "I really shouldn't be eating this." You're anxious. You're indecisive. You're standing up. You're going back for more. All your brain ever records are tiny, insignificant, paper-thin pieces. But, your hips and thighs are somehow *less* fooled when you come in 20 minutes later, and to your shock and horror *three-quarters* of the pie is gone—and yet you still feel thoroughly unsatisfied. The visual scarcity that your brain registered during the actual (repeated) eating experience never allowed you to achieve emotional satisfaction. Whereas, if you had taken that same, three-fourths of the *entire* pie, put it on a plate, and sat down to peacefully eat it (with whipped cream), you would have felt thoroughly satisfied *psychologically*—and stopped after a much smaller portion.

Plate size matters

One of the key problems with psychological satisfaction is that your mind can play tricks on you. Interestingly enough, the size of the plate you use *directly* impacts the amount of food required to feel mentally satisfied. To examine this point, researchers gave subjects two different-sized bowls and unlimited access to cereal. The participants with the large bowls ate significantly more cereal than those with the smaller bowls. Okay, not surprising, right? But get this, when asked to rate the amount of cereal they consumed, the people with the large bowl estimated that they ate *far less* than those with the small bowl. So, a larger plate not only makes you eat more but it makes you *think* you've eaten much less—now that's one high-calorie optical illusion!

Use a smaller plate

When food is served in a smaller bowl, your brain actually registers it as more food. If you put two cups of popcorn in a huge salad serving bowl—the big one you'd use to serve a party of six—the kernels would scarcely fill the bottom, leaving tons of empty space. But, if you took the same two cups of popcorn and put it in a small ice cream bowl, it would be brimming over the top in a nice plentiful mound, making the same amount of popcorn look like so much more.

So you may want to swap out those chic oversized dinner plates—that dwarf your meal with the abundant white space in the background—for a salad plate. I use beautiful china salad plates as my dinner plates. The smaller plates still hold an ample amount for me to feel satisfied, and the food extends to the edges, with a smaller white space-to-food ratio, which triggers a psychological sense of abundance. I invite you to play around with different sized plates to see how you experience these benefits as well.

Small, but not too small

There is, however, a tipping point. If you use too small of a container, the pendulum swings the other direction and it triggers a sense of lack and dissatisfaction. For example, if you use a small ramekin for something really tiny like chocolate chips or a few malt balls, it's great. But if you serve ice cream in that same micro-mini bowl, it could look far *too* small and you would feel deprived. (More about this in Habit #5, below.) So play around with it and find the sizes that work best for you. As a general guideline, it's great to start with salad plates for your meal, and smaller dainty bowls for cereal, ice cream, etc. Let your sense of abundance (and deprivation) guide you.

Plating your food makes mindless second helpings less likely–or at the very least, a conscious choice

Another benefit of putting your entire meal out in front of you on a plate (dessert included), is that if you are full but still have that nagging Non-Hunger Desire to eat, you actually have to get up in order to get more. Whereas, if you're just sitting there eating out of the bag—and you get to the point where you've had enough, but the only effort it's going to take to eat more is to extend your wrist two inches farther into the bag to grab another handful—it's going to be a lot easier to keep eating. By creating a scenario where you need to physically get up, go in the kitchen, and deliberately serve yourself more, it gives you the time to interrupt the process. You can take that moment to check in, to make sure, "Is this what I really want to be doing?"

Putting your entire serving on a plate significantly enhances your ability to visually register the abundance of your meal, while eating it off a smaller plate further amplifies your satisfaction by maximizing the perceived amount of what's there. And finally, the actual act—itself—of plating your food adds that third supportive element, creating a physical and psychological distance that gives you space to purposefully decide whether you get a second helping.

Habit #4: Take a Substantial Portion

This next habit likely flies in the face of everything you've ever been told about how to eat to get thin. Diet gurus are constantly admonishing you to "watch your portions," and "cut down on portion size." But as we've just seen in Habit #3's *Commit to what you're eating*, when you keep running back and forth between the freezer and the couch for a single spoonful of ice cream—you end up eating a significant amount, yet are still left unsatisfied.

In fact, while a smaller (but not *too* small) plate does make the brain perceive the same portion size of something as a larger volume of food, this concept has a significant tipping point. When foods are presented in what is perceived to be too small of a package, the *exact opposite* reaction occurs. This scenario makes the same volume of food appear to be much less. A study conducted at Arizona State University and the University of Kentucky shows that dieters will actually eat more food, and consume more total calories if the portions are presented in smaller sizes or smaller packages. (Take that diet-indoctrinators!) The researchers put a 200-calorie serving of regular-size M&M's into one regular-size plastic sandwich bag, and then they took the 200-calorie equivalent serving of mini M&M's and divided them into four (smaller) snack-size plastic bags. This simulated the (single-serving) packs of cookies and crackers you see marketed so frequently as "100-calorie snack-sized." When they studied how this packaging affected the total amount people ate, and perceived that they ate, they found two very interesting things.

First, even though there was the *exact same number* of calories in both scenarios, people perceived the mini M&M's in four smaller packages to be more like diet food. Which they then rated as a negative eating experience overall. Yet, while they stereotyped the mini packs of M&M's as feeling like diet food, they evaluated them as having *more* calories. An internal conflict arose for the subjects because they thought that the mini M&M's were both diet food, which is negative, and higher in caloric content, which is a no-no if they were dieting. So when presented with the four smaller individual packages—even though they contained the *exact same number of calories* as the one larger bag—it actually created anxiety and stress for the dieters. (And tell me, who on earth needs more stress because of the way their M&M's are packaged, right?) As if the anxiety wasn't enough, eating the four smaller packages triggered the Eating Cuz You Ate response, because they believed that they had overdone it and broken their diet. So eating the perceived smaller portion left them feeling stressed, deprived, and throwing in the towel because they figured they'd already blown it. Yeah… can you say backfire?

The take-home message from these poor tortured participants of the M&M's study is this: When you're hungry and dishing up your meal—*take a substantial portion.* In fact, err on the side of taking a large-ish portion to put on your plate. We'll soon see in Chapter 7 how leaving food behind on your plate is actually incredibly beneficial. So, you can ditch all that extra packaging and expense of those well-intentioned 100-calorie packs, because they actually make you feel worse *and* eat more.

Habit #5: Make Your Meal Visually Appealing

Another way to turbocharge your satisfaction is by turning your meal into a visual masterpiece. This is easily accomplished with a little imagination: Serve your snack on a beautiful dish with a placemat, or fan out a sliced strawberry on the side of the plate. A lot of time we eat to feel a sense of indulgence, or to feel nurtured, or pampered. So while you're actually hungry, why not make eating the *most* enjoyable dignified experience possible? Go ahead and splash a few sweet and refreshing orange slices and a sprig of mint into your water, transforming it into an elevated indulgence.

People have really had a lot of fun writing in to me about this one. One woman pulled out her china that had been sitting in the cupboards for years, and started using it—*bewildered* that it never occurred to her to do so before. Another woman placed fresh-cut roses at the table while she was eating. Someone else wrote that the simple act of slicing her sandwich on the diagonal, instead of straight up and down, made it seem so much more posh and special. So, while laying your full meal out in front of you, have fun with making the entire eating experience as visually pleasing as possible.

What's one thing that you could do today to make your eating experience more of a visual work of art? Start a running list and keep your eye out for the things you notice in magazines, blogs, and restaurants that will make your eating experience have more visual *zing*.

Habit #6: Be Present

Eat while you're eating. This habit takes eating without distractions to the next level. I encourage you to avoid doing other things, like watching TV, talking on the phone, working on the computer, or reading a book or magazine—and to focus solely on your meal while you are eating. Concentrating on your food promotes naturally thin eating in two ways. First, if you're doing other things, you're going to be distracted, and therefore not able to fully enjoy the food or recognize when you're full. Then, when your body has had enough, your brain still protests, "Hey wait, we've hardly had anything!" The other benefit of not engaging in other endeavors while eating is that it eliminates those conditioned Pavlovian triggers. So, if you're not doing anything else while you're eating, you're going to be extinguishing—and *not creating* (any new)—environmental triggers that activate Non-Hunger Eating. Since you'll no longer be pairing your day-to-day activities with food. And finally, the data is conclusive: One of the chief goals of emotional eating is to escape self-awareness. (Which is just "psychology speak" for zoning out.) So, you also get a kick-start on eliminating the Mean Girl Munchies and other types of emotional eating simply by staying present while you're eating.

So, how do you do it? The first step to being present while you're eating is to limit distractions. Sit in your Designated Eating Spot. Make sure the TV's off, hold your calls, and don't text or read. *Just eat.* The interesting thing is that by "restricting" these other activities, you'll notice you ironically start Gasping to do them. Which is great, because you'll have something pulling you toward an activity once you've reached satisfaction.

Staying focused while eating with others

If you're eating with others, you might want to save stressful or tense conversations for later. At first, eating with another person, in and of itself, can be a significant distraction. So one thing my clients have found really useful is that when you're about to eat with others, take a moment at the beginning of the meal and really anchor to the fact that you're eating while being social. Have a little (internal) pre-meal talk with yourself: *OK, you're eating, you're going to be talking with people, and that can be a little distracting. So remember every now and again to come back inside of yourself to relax and just check in with your satisfaction. Remember to taste the food and enjoy both the conversation and what you're eating.*

If eating with others feels like a challenge, you may want to ease into that. At first, you might feel more comfortable having a few meals by yourself (when possible) so you can practice awareness, and then slowly transition into eating with others—as you feel more relaxed and confident.

Navigating the perils of a shared dessert

Diet books often prompt you to split a meal or share a dessert as a way of decreasing portion size. This is a fine idea, unless, while you're dipping your fork in to take the perfect bite of that amazing chocolate cake and slowly putting it in your mouth, letting the ganache explode on your tongue, the person you're sharing it with is shoveling three-fourths of it into their mouth in a single (colossal) bite. That is going to trigger a five-alarm *very* valid sense of deprivation. It doesn't take a genius to realize that if you don't pick up the pace, the food really will be gone—faster than you can say, "Hey! I thought we were *sharing!*"

When you're splitting something, it's going to be incredibly tempting to eat quickly to ensure you get your share. Here's an easy fix. Take your portion and put it on your own plate. This way, you'll still get the benefits of a shared serving, but with the added *perk* that the other person can pitchfork their entire helping of cake directly into their mouth without an ounce of impact on your eating ease. You're left free to linger on each purposeful bite and savor it to maximum satisfaction.

Eat at the speed that matches your hunger

Another way to be present while you're eating is to slow down, although only to the extent that it doesn't feel like deprivation. A lot of intuitive eating books tell you to eat really slowly; even going as far as to tell you the number of times you should chew each bite. But imposing a speed limit can fuel restrictive tension. Eating quickly isn't necessarily a bad thing. In fact, a study that compared the eating speed of dieters and non-dieters found that when very hungry, both groups ate rather swiftly at the start of a meal. The difference showed up when they approached satisfaction. The non-dieters dramatically decreased the speed at which they ate once they started to approach fullness. However, as dieters approached feeling full, they kept on steadily eating at the same rapid pace. Which makes perfect sense when you consider all the Gasping for Food going on in their heads. So play around with being mindful of your speed. When you start to approach feeling satisfied, notice if you slow down or get nervous and speed up. If you *do* find yourself speeding up, it may be a sign of anxiousness. In which case, you can calmly assure yourself that even though this meal is over, it's just for now—the delicious food isn't going anywhere.

Rumination-Free Meals

Have you ever been eating and suddenly noticed that you're kind of angrily stabbing at your food with your fork? You realize that you'd completely lost awareness of your meal—and were replaying a stressful conversation in your head? Rumination is a serious threat to meal satisfaction. The word ruminating comes from the term describing how cows regurgitate and re-chew what they've eaten—chewing their cud. But for us, it isn't grass. It's negative experiences, conversations or unresolved problems that our mind is re-chewing. It's when you painfully rehash and repeatedly go over something that is bothering you—replaying its causes and predicting the (usually negative) consequences. Many times people tend to think about their stressful concerns about overeating itself, while they're eating!

Rumination pairs two cognitive practices: reflection and brooding. You find yourself replaying the frustrating thing that happened at work, in a negative, repetitious manner. Reflection is quite useful when paired with action-oriented solution seeking. It is when reflection is paired with worry-charged brooding that it becomes counterproductive. When we do this aloud with a girlfriend, it's called venting. This actually leads to much more stress—and sadly, not just for you—for *both* parties. It also leads to a more pronounced depressed mood. Feeling stressed and depressed are bad enough, but those aren't even the reasons rumination made the list. *Rumination can be powerfully distracting.* It can suck you into a negative, painful, zoned-out space where you suddenly look down—and the entire pot of mac and cheese has unexpectedly disappeared.

When you ruminate, you'll notice your eating takes on a methodic repetitious motion. Your focus has left the food. Your stomach will often feel tight, tensely clenched high up into your chest. This is not the ideal scenario for relaxing and checking in with your stomach to see if you're satisfied. So once you notice you're chewing your mental cud, it helps to take a deep breath and unclench your stomach, so the food can more easily register with your brain. Second, write down what it is you're concerned about, and assure yourself that you can resolve it when your meal is done.

Habit #7: Construct and Savor the Perfect Bite—Every Time

Did you ever get busted as a child for playing with your food? Well guess what, I'm inviting you to do just that. I encourage you to get into the habit of crafting each and every bite that goes into your mouth. Make it *exactly* how you like it. Cut off the outer portion so that you get the succulent inner piece you really want. If you're eating a taco salad, make sure that you get lettuce, guacamole, sour cream, beans, and crispy taco strips—in every bite. Cut out the heart of the watermelon, or that center gooey spiral of the cinnamon roll. Make each bite exactly what you want.

Eat the best part first

Dieters save the very best part—the frosting on the cupcake, or the thick, doughy fold of pizza—to eat *last*. Whereas, naturally thin eaters dive in and eat the best part first. Enjoying the best part first is a very smart strategy. Since eating is going to take place within the relatively small window between hunger and fullness, you want to make sure you eat the best parts while you're actually *hungry*, because the best parts will taste the most blow-your-mind-amazing when your senses are still heightened by real physical hunger. So that way, as you approach satisfaction—and your taste superpowers start to fade—all that remains are the less desirable bits that you've already picked over while crafting your succulent bites. And you'll be able to push aside *those* mangled scraps much more easily. If you notice you're feeling full after eating only the bottom of the (kinda dry) cupcake, but what you really love is the rich cream cheese frosting, it's going to be much more difficult to end the meal when the delectable ivory swirls are still left—staring up at you.

To truly maximize the enjoyment of your food when entering into a new eating experience, simply taste everything that's on your plate, and see which things you like most. Decide where you want to focus your eating attention during this meal. And then, go ahead and eat those best parts first.

So now that you've shut off distractions, beautifully displayed a substantial portion on your reasonably sized salad plate, and sat in your Designated Eating Spot to enjoy your meal, you're ready to explore the keys to effortlessly stop eating when you're comfortably satisfied.

chapter seven

THE MILLION DOLLAR THIN SKILL

How to Stop Eating When You've Had Enough Fuel—
The Secret to Ending Any Meal With Ease

STEP 4: HOW TO STOP EATING WHEN YOU'RE COMFORTABLY SATISFIED

You're about to learn how to stop eating when you feel comfortably satisfied. Total cinch, right? If Step 2, *Eat What You Really, Really Want*, is the skill that causes the most terror in people, Step 4, *How to Stop When You're Comfortably Satisfied*, is the one that can cause the most frustration. In this chapter you'll get the tools and information you need to easily—from the inside out—push the food away when you've had enough.

We talked earlier about how each of the five steps work together. Each one by itself is difficult, but when implemented together, they work synergistically, seamlessly catapulting you toward success. This is perhaps the most true with stopping when you're satisfied. Think about it. If physical hunger isn't what launched your current eating episode, then how in the world is feeling satisfied going to be what signals you to stop? Hunger and fullness are like two bookends. If hunger is what starts you eating, then feeling satisfied would naturally be what makes it easy to stop. However, if feeling frustrated with a project at work is what initiated your eating, then what is your signal to stop? When the problem is solved? When the chips and salsa are gone? When you hear someone coming down the hall?

So, if you're feeling anxious about your ability to let go of food when you've had enough, remember that each one of these steps builds you up for success in the next. If you're physically hungry when you decide to eat, choose what you really want, and then sit down and consciously enjoy each bite, you'll be beautifully setting yourself up to stop eating when you feel satisfied.

WHAT DOES SATISFACTION FEEL LIKE?

Have you been eating by calorie counts and glycemic index lists for so long that you have no idea what it *experientially* feels like to approach satisfaction? Before we explore the four reasons why you would ever eat past full, and learn the seven ways to end a meal with ease, it's important to answer the obvious question—*How on earth do I know when I've had enough food?* If your past has been checkered with dieting and painful out-of-control eating, it's very likely you feel nervous at times that you'll eat too much. (Sometimes even afraid that you won't be able to stop.) This end-of-meal anxiety that creeps up can interfere with your body's natural signals, making it difficult to know what feeling comfortably satisfied actually feels like.

The first sign of satisfaction is a slight dip in taste.

The first response your body sends to indicate you've consumed enough fuel is something that dieters often tragically misread. You'll recall from Step 1 that physical hunger is the ideal cue to start eating, because your sense of smell and taste are dramatically heightened. Your hunger-induced bionic nose can smell In-N-Out Burger three cities away, and when you eat, the food detonates delectable fireworks of flavor in your mouth. Well, satisfaction uses that very same mechanism. The first indication that you're approaching satiation is that the taste of the food starts to diminish—just slightly.

Chasing the Taste

Dieters unfortunately respond to this dip in taste very differently than naturally thin eaters. When a dieter is enjoying the intense pleasure of a meal and she notices the potency of flavor start to diminish, not wanting it to end—she starts "chasing the taste." Her eating pace quickens in an attempt to recapture the pleasurable sensation that is beginning to fade. But it is a futile quest. The more she eats trying to chase the high she experienced at the start of the meal, the fuller she gets, thus pushing the sought after pleasure even farther away. "Maybe I just need to eat something else," she reasons as the heightened flavor persists in eluding her. "How about something salty?" She munches a few Smoke-house almonds. No flavor explosion. "Maybe something sweet will do the trick?" She nibbles on a few caramel rice cakes. "No, still not what I was looking for." But the only way to restore that flavor-pleasure intensity is to let her body get hungry again. It was the hunger—not the food itself—that created the fever pitch of flavor in the first place.

Recognizing that flavor diminishes as you near fullness becomes even more significant as you master waiting for physical hunger. I remember years ago, near the very beginning of my journey, I got really good at waiting for hunger—so of course pretty much whatever I ate tasted sensational. But as I approached satisfaction the taste would start to slip away. I had no idea that the flavor intensity was a direct function of my hunger level. So, I'd clumsily grasp for that taste high, like a wet bar of soap. The more I'd reach for it, the farther away it slipped. I would sample a wide array of foods seeking that almighty flavor zip. But everything I tasted would fall flat. What was even more insidious was that I'd eat so much on my flavor-quest that I'd get disappointed and would be tempted to beat myself up—promptly moving from Chasing the Taste to Eating Cuz You Ate. And it just wasn't pretty.

Being physically hungry is the *only* way to invoke the bionic power to experience the heightened taste sensation. But as you start to feel satisfied, you're going lose your olfactory super powers, and food's going to go back to tasting mediocre. Which is actually wonderful, because when the food tastes less desirable, it's so much easier to push it away when you've had enough.

HOW MUCH FOOD WILL
IT TAKE TO FEEL SATISFIED?

We're so used to relying on the meal measurements of sample diet menus—pulled from glossy magazine pages—that we're left hazy about the actual volume of food our body really needs. A question I'm frequently asked is, "How much food will it take to feel satisfied?" Well, the answer is... it depends. It depends on what you last ate, when you last ate, and what you've been doing in between. If you ate a small bowl of cereal five hours ago and you're a mail carrier running around nonstop, your body's going to need a significant amount of food to get your fuel supply back up. Whereas if you polished off a personal pizza the size of a hubcap two hours ago, and you work in an office where you've been sitting at your desk all day, you likely won't need to eat again for a while.

Ultimately, you don't need to worry about portion size at all, because your body is going to tell you the exact amount you need by communicating with you through the drop in taste. It's likely that you'll be very surprised at how much less food it takes for you to actually feel satisfied. Less than you probably imagined. Especially when what you're eating is succulent, real, normal food, and it's what you *really* wanted. You're going to feel deeply satisfied and have a heightened taste experience while you're losing weight. The ultimate trifecta.

To explore how much fuel your body needs, you can start out eating half of what you normally used to eat. You can use that as a place to take a break and really check in to see if your body is adequately nourished. There are two caveats to this. First, this only applies if overeating is something that you've struggled with in the past. If under-eating has been your challenge, cutting your existing portions in half is not going to serve you. Second, if plating only a half portion feels like deprivation, go ahead and put that full serving on the plate to capture the visual abundance and still check in with yourself after you've eaten half of the food.

THE FOUR REASONS YOU'D EVER EAT PAST FULL

So, why then is it so hard to stop eating sometimes? Four reasons really. You'd only ever miss, override, or ignore your body's signal to stop eating as the result of: deprivation, distraction, distress, or inertia.

1. Deprivation

If you've restricted carbs for six weeks straight and you're finally eating a doughy, thick-crusted piece of real Chicago deep-dish pizza (which you *know* you're not going to let yourself have again anytime soon) you quickly put up your mental "Do Not Disturb" sign. You're *so* not going to let those pesky little satisfaction signals interrupt this bliss. No way! You're going to eat all you can, because there is no knowing when you'll be allowed such flavorful fare again. Makes perfect sense. The Gasping for Food response is a powerful trigger to override your physiological satiety signals. This eating is not about hunger. It's about scarcity. You want to get as much as you can while the floodgates are open. This is why when you diet you feel such a strong pull to keep eating certain foods long past satisfaction—with the same ferocity with which they had been restricted. (Happily, HDE eliminates these devious effects of deprivation.)

2. Distraction

A recent study at the University of Bellingham unleashed a man dressed in a yellow and purple clown suit with polka-dot sleeves, red shoes, and a huge bulbous red nose riding a unicycle into the central courtyard. When researchers questioned students crossing the square if they had seen anything unusual, 92% of the students talking on cell phones completely missed the unicycling clown circling a few feet in front of them. People engrossed in a mobile phone conversation experience a phenomenon called "inattentional blindness"—they look at their surroundings but none of it registers. When you are distracted while eating you could call it *"intestinal* blindness"—you're eating, but nothing you consume registers on your fullness scale.

Distraction makes it easy to eat more than your body needs by obscuring both physical and psychological satisfaction signals. If something shiny has your attention, you fail to register the amount, quality, and fabulousness of what you're eating. Which is an essential component to achieving mental satiation. Additionally, as we talked about in Step 3, engaging in other activities while you're eating can make your body's polite satisfaction signals as invisible as the clown on the unicycle.

3. Distress

Let's get clear about this. If you are using food in any given moment as a way to soothe or escape emotional pain—hunger has nothing to do with that equation. Consequently, fullness or satisfaction will have absolutely no bearing on your eating at that time. (Well, other than possibly piling on more distress because you feel so upset that you ate when you weren't hungry.) And while the main goal of emotional eating is to check out and disconnect from difficult feelings, unfortunately, you also unintentionally end up disconnecting from your other (helpful) bodily senses—which makes it extremely easy to bypass the signs of real satisfaction.

4. Inertia

Okay so do you remember Newton's First Law of Motion: An object in motion tends to stay in motion unless an external force is applied to it? Well, when you are eating, you are like an object set in motion. A very pleasant motion, at that. Transitioning from eating to a different activity requires a shift of direction. If you are going from a highly pleasurable act, like eating, to a neutral or worse yet, dreaded task, like doing the dishes or a demanding work project, it is going to take one powerful external force to break the magnetic pleasure-pull inertia of food.

Transitions

Transition times tend to pose a sizeable challenge when it comes to non-hunger eating. It's very common to find yourself mindlessly munching when you're transitioning from one part of your day to another. Like when you get home from a stressful day at work, or after you finally get the baby down, or making it to a long-awaited break in lengthy day of classes. When changing gears from one activity to another, people often experience an urge to release the anxiety that has been building over the day—and eating becomes the go-to pressure release valve. One particularly challenging transition is at the end of a meal. You may find yourself feeling apprehensive as you start nearing physical satisfaction because you're not ready for the emotional pleasure of eating to end. There are seven strategies that will effectively assist you in expertly navigating this juncture, and will set you up to end your meals like a pro.

THE SEVEN TECHNIQUES
TO END ANY MEAL WITH EASE

If food only seems to tighten its grip when you try to push it away, here are seven tips that will make transitioning out of your meals a breeze.

1. Plan for Post-Meal Pleasure

Eating is pleasurable, or at the very least, pleasantly engaging. If you're planning to do a chore that you've been dreading after you finish your meal—like going back to work on a really stressful project, mopping the kitchen floor, or even just not having *anything* planned—it is going to be infinitely more difficult to swap out the pleasure of eating for something odious, or even just blah.

One way to skip over the end of meal doldrums is by having an engaging activity planned for the few minutes immediately following your meal. Pick something that you genuinely really enjoy doing and save it for right after your meals. Get really clear about what the diversion will be *before* you eat. The more concrete and mapped-out the endeavor, the better. It doesn't need to be a huge time investment. If you have a hectic schedule, it can be something you do for five indulgent minutes.

You can create positive tension to drive up the allure of your after-meal pleasurable activity by using the Gasping principle. So, as you've seen whenever you restrict something, you create a heightened desire for it. You can now use this motivational truth for good as opposed to evil. By restricting your post-meal activity, and *only* allowing yourself to engage in it when you're transitioning out of a meal, you will create an environment where the activity is so enticing that you *can't wait* to finish your meal. So, if you have a guilty-pleasure magazine or blog you love reading or a new episode of a show you're eager to watch, don't let yourself read it or watch it. Absolutely (playfully) forbid those activities *except* for right after you eat.

Restricting your post-meal activity amps up the excitement to enter into it. It facilitates a seamless transition from eating, which is pleasurable, to your post-meal activity, which is now even *more* pleasurable because you're Gasping for it! Having something to look forward to that is as enjoyable as eating (with tension built up around it) makes it a snap to push away from the table when you're satisfied.

2. Use a Timer

You know that place during a meal where you start to feel satisfied and that terrible, nervous chatter pipes up? "Oh no, you really should stop eating now." And the other voice rebels, "No, I still want more." "Stop!" "No, I don't want to!" And you spiral into the maddening Eat-It/Don't-Eat-It tug of war. You can cleverly navigate your way around that battlefield with an unlikely weapon—a timer. A simple kitchen or phone timer is all you need. Pressuring yourself to stop eating only increases the intensity of the desire to *keep* eating, escalating a battle dependent on the brute force of your will. And if you're tired or distracted, you're going to lose. But with a little inventive meal transition judo, you can easily emerge the victor—and bypass the entire battle.

Rather than bullying yourself into ending the meal, you simple press pause. Then, in your most reassuring tone, have a little talk with yourself, "I'm going to set this timer for five minutes, and if in five minutes you still want to eat this food, hungry or not, I'm going to let you have it."

Next you set the timer for five minutes, leave your eating location and *do something*. Freeze your meal in your mind and go actively engage in another activity (possibly your post-meal pleasurable activity) for five minutes—doing something is key. Mentally dive headfirst into an activity. And eighty-five to ninety percent of the time, when that timer goes off, you'll find yourself momentarily baffled, unable to remember why you set it. By using the timer you create a space where it's possible to completely forget about the food. Because you gave yourself full permission to eat in five minutes, you diffused the sense of deprivation, pausing it long enough to shift your focus and launch your inertia into your next activity. And without even knowing it, you will successfully transition.

3. Leave Food Behind on Your Plate

Our brains really are brilliant—but oddly enough, are *easily* tricked when it comes to certain things. True brilliance is when we learn to use those cognitive loopholes to our advantage. This third tip is one that I love, love, love. This meal-ending marvel is simply to leave some food behind on your plate. And don't just leave a teensy scrap; leave a succulent, delicious, quality bite. This little trick does two impressive things.

First, it communicates loud and clear who's in charge. It firmly declares, "Hey food, I'm in charge of *you*, you're not the boss of me. I'm the one that decides. I can take you or I can leave you." This is a *very* different message than you may have inadvertently communicated in the past. Like those times you may have felt a little powerless while under the pull of that chocolate raised donut. (I've been there. It's no fun!) When I first started eating this way, I left a quality bite of every single thing I ate (and sometimes even some of my beverage). This mightily boosts your sense of self-efficacy and personal power, visually reinforcing that you have the freedom to choose, and that you are the one in charge.

Second, leaving food behind on your plate dramatically reduces the likelihood that you'll go back for seconds. Letting some food remain on your plate triggers your brain to register a sense of abundance, which plays a powerful role in psychological satisfaction. This abundance mentality is the exact opposite of deprivation. This physical representation of surplus will send the subtle message to your brain—*surely if I left something on the plate, then I've had enough. I don't need more.* Whereas if you always eat until the plate is empty, the chance of you going back for seconds or thirds is much higher. This one little action has such a considerable impact that I invite you to try it out for yourself. So, after taking a significant portion of what you're wanting to eat, simply take a generous bite of whatever you're eating, put it over to the side and leave it there. Then when you get up to clear your plate, notice how empowered you feel—and take a minute to anchor the feeling of ease it lends to transitioning out of the meal.

4. Rate the Taste

Measuring things that can't be objectively perceived, like satisfaction, can be challenging, but it's a great way to get a more concrete handle on them. You'll recall that the first sign your body has obtained enough fuel is that the taste starts to diminish. So, a really good way to create a more tangible anchor for satisfaction is to Rate the Taste. Simply rate the deliciousness of what you are eating from One to Ten, where One means the food is completely uninteresting, and Ten means it's pure bliss. To start, take your baseline measurement of your first bite—which hopefully is going to be a Ten. If your first bite's not a Ten, that indicates one of two things: a) you weren't very hungry when you started eating, or b) that you didn't quite pick what it was that you were wanting. Both are fine, and are absolutely going to happen. This is a process. You're learning. And even when you've got it mastered—life isn't perfect. There are going to be anomalies.

So, you sit down, take that first bite and it's a Nine or Ten. Amazing, it's an explosion of flavor in your mouth. Then you simply check back in every few minutes and consciously rate the taste again. "Where am I at? Is it a Nine, is it an Eight?" And when you get down to a Seven, that's usually a great place to stop. But remember, this is a *guideline* to help you connect with your sense of satisfaction. This is not a rule. The minute it becomes a rule you unleash the chatter of, "Oh my gosh, you're at a Seven, you need to stop! Stop! Oh no. You're not stopping!" Turning this into a rule also opens the door to Eating Cuz You Ate the minute you eat past that Seven and get to the Six. That is in no way the goal. The goal is to help you assess where you're at so that once you get to Seven, you can really notice from the inside out, "Hey, this actually doesn't taste as good as it did just minutes ago when I first started eating."

Realizing the taste has weakened makes it so much easier to push the food away. Then the very next time that you're hungry, a few hours later, when you take that first bite it's going to be a symphonic Level Ten crescendo of flavor again. By Rating the Taste you reinforce experientially the fact that you never need to Chase the Taste. The flavor zing reliably returns the very next time you're hungry. This will help you really relax, and make it a whole lot easier to stop eating when the taste drops to a Seven. Because you'll know that all you have to do is wait a little while for hunger, and it will again be soaring at a Ten.

Another way to quantify satisfaction is to use the five-point hunger scale from Step 1. In addition to using the scale to assess your hunger, you can use it on the back end to measure satiation as well. So you simply determine where your hunger is at the beginning of the meal and continue to check in to see when it has dropped down to a Three or Two, where you are comfortably satisfied. It can take a few minutes for your blood sugar to register and send a satisfaction signal. Therefore using the Hunger Scale isn't quite as immediate an indicator of fullness as Rating the Taste. It is a good alternative to Rating the Taste however, if you're finding that you're getting caught up in the "Oh my gosh, am I at a Six? Or am I at a Seven?" indecision. If you find that you're getting a little nervous or hyper-focused when you Rate the Taste, that's when you might want to take a step back and use the broader Hunger Scale to rate your satisfaction.

5. Ask the Next-Bite Question

It's very likely that you spend a lot of energy worrying about food and your weight—but ultimately where the rubber hits the road, every time, is the single decision about the next bite. As you approach the point of satisfaction while eating, there's a powerful question you can ask yourself: "Is this next bite going to make me feel better, or slightly worse—physically, mentally, emotionally?" Your entire relationship with food comes down to those single bite moments. This question collapses all your thoughts about food down to one simple question. "By moving my wrist from my plate to my mouth and taking this next bite, will I be moving myself in a direction that benefits me? Is it going to be nurturing, supporting, satisfying? Or, by that action am I going to be moving myself in the direction of pain? Am I going to feel physically uncomfortable if I take this next bite? Am I going to feel emotionally distressed and disappointed?" **The Next Bite Question: "Will this next bite make me feel better or worse?"** is a great way to bring your focus to the defining moment that makes the difference.

6. Create an End-of-Meal Routine

We are creatures of habit. Do you notice that once you start your morning routine, brushing your teeth, taking a shower, putting on your makeup—that your morning sort of goes on autopilot? The sixth technique uses the momentum of routine to effortlessly propel you through eating and well into your next activity. It's especially useful if the ritual gets you away from the food. Some people like to get up and go brush their teeth, because they notice that the minty taste really changes the environment in their mouth, and makes it a lot less likely that they're going to want to go back and munch on something savory afterwards. Washing the dishes you've used is a pragmatic option. A 10-minute brisk walk is a stellar choice. Play around with the activity that works best for you. One that clearly marks that mealtime is over.

Having a ritual set up around ending your meal helps you transition in three major ways. First, it puts an end cap on the experience. A lot of us—especially before we mastered sit, silverware, and savor (the Three S's)—didn't really have a formal beginning or ending to our eating. Our day was kind of this long intermittent stream of eating. By actually committing to a plate and sitting down, you have a clear beginning mark of your meal. And now, by implementing an end-of-meal ritual, you're going to have a clear end mark as well.

Second, an end-of-meal routine uses the power of Pavlovian conditioning. Remember how by pairing the bell with food, eventually Pavlov's dogs would salivate whenever the bell rang? Even when the food was *not* present. When you pair a ritual such as washing the dishes, reading a few pages of a book, or brushing your teeth with the end of your meal, you're training your brain to register that you're done eating. The end-of-meal activity starts to act as a Pavlovian trigger that pops you out of the mood to eat, and primes the urge and expectation for what is next.

And third, an end-of-meal routine helps smoothly transition you into your next activity—because you'll know what's coming next. As we talked about in Technique 1, there's a tendency to linger at your meal when you don't have anything positive following it. Planning end-of-meal pleasure is a useful tool, but it takes a lot of work to create excitement. Planning post-meal pleasure is really helpful at the beginning of this process, or when you find yourself going through some trouble periods, or paired with specific foods that are initially hard to let go of. However, instituting consistent and doable fun events for the end of every meal can take a significant amount effort and forethought. An end-of-meal *routine*, on the other hand, is an easier option for everyday use, enabling you to set it and forget it. It puts the end-of-meal transition on autopilot, so you don't even think about it.

7. Out of Sight, Out of Mind–and Mouth

There is something to be said for the old adage "Out of sight, out of mind." Clearing the food, and/or removing yourself from the premises when you start to feel satisfied, eliminates exposure to the visual prompts to continue eating. This is much easier to accomplish when you're at home, where you have control over the eating environment. However, when you're eating out, and you've gotten to that point where you feel satisfied, but the food is still on the table and people are lingering and talking, you can do one of three things. First, you can ask the waitstaff to take your food away and box it up for later.

While removing the leftover food from your field of vision is usually the best option, there are instances where it's just not feasible. If you're full, but the server is nowhere to be found, and the rest of the buttery sour-cream-slathered baked potato is incessantly calling to you from your plate, you can simply take your napkin and cover it. Sometimes drastic times call for drastic measures—and you're the boss, fully allowed to step in for yourself and assert your authority (especially in the case of an emergency). If the food pull is particularly troublesome, you can simply destroy it. Swivel the lid off the shaker and give the remainders a pepper bath. If you're dining with people you don't feel totally comfortable with, you can always do this in a more discreet manner. Or give it a hot chili sauce treatment. So, when you're out at a restaurant and the food is sitting there calling to you after you feel satisfied, feel free to take matters into your own hands and "season" it into submission.

You are now armed and ready to become the eighth wonder of the world: a person who can stop halfway through a piece of cake when she's comfortably satisfied.

chapter eight

WILLPOWER, WANTPOWER & INSIDE-OUT NUTRITION

The Key to Truly Craving
What is Actually Good for You

STEP 5: CHECK IN TO SEE
HOW THE FOOD MAKES YOU FEEL

O kay, by this point you might be thinking, "Great, Hunger Directed Eating! I can eat whatever I want and get, and stay, thin—*but can that be healthy?*" Well, if this is your question, first let me say that you are a *far* better person than I am. Back in the day when my eating was really nutty, if someone had said I could eat *whatever* I wanted—and I'd get and stay thin—I would have been on board even if it was incredibly unhealthy. Are you kidding me? When I think of the insane things I tried back in my dieting days, it was clear that health was not my driving force. This is why, years later, I am still a tad gobsmacked that I now consistently eat healthier than I ever conceived possible. Step 5, *Check In to See How the Food Makes You Feel,* is the nutritional secret weapon that enables you to eat a very healthful, balanced assortment of foods that are perfect for *your* body.

The icing on the Hunger Directed Eating cake, however, is the delightful paradox that by *allowing* yourself Donuts and Doritos you end up consistently eating *more nutritiously* than you ever imagined attainable—from the inside out. Without willpower. Or a dietician. You'll naturally gravitate toward nutrient-rich foods because those will be what you really, really want. There are only two reasons you'd ever fill your body with suboptimal fuel. (Well, *three* if you count temporary situations where you subsist on airport or gas station food on a cross-country trip.) The first reason is what we've covered extensively—that you've inadvertently created a powerful magnetic attraction towards unhealthy foods by restricting them. The second reason you'd fill your tank with low-grade fuel is that constant diet-induced food chatter has disconnected you from your body's nutrition-seeking system. This is actually excellent news. Your body can be trusted—truly. You aren't addicted to food. You don't have a deep psychological desire to self-sabotage your weight-loss goals. You've simply been trying to solve the problem (excess weight) with a solution (dieting) that *exacerbates the symptoms* (Non-Hunger Eating). And another side effect of the faulty dieting "solution" is that your body's natural preference for wholesome foods gets lost in the crazy, deprivation, craving, dieting shuffle.

By initially allowing your food choices to be influenced by your nutrient-sparse, diet-induced Kryptonite cravings, these foods are quickly stripped of their powerful pull (and allure). Less pull means you'll eat them less. This alone dramatically (and favorably) alters the nutritional balance of your daily fare. Which is great. But wait, there's more. Normalizing previously forbidden "naughty foods" results in you eating these unwholesome foods *less*—while Step 5 results in you eating nutritionally optimal foods *more*. It may sound like I'm splitting hairs, but there is an important difference. Losing interest in deep-fried Snickers bars is one thing. But *gaining* interest in wholesome, nutrient-rich whole foods is another thing entirely. Step 5, *Check In to See How the Food Makes You Feel*, reconnects you with the aspect of your body's thin-telligence that leads you to crave the custom-selected foods that provide your body with optimum fuel. You'll be the most surprised person in the room as you notice yourself naturally reaching for nourishing foods—because you genuinely *want* them. Not only will Step 5 revolutionize your nutrition, it's actually the easiest of all five steps.

In this chapter you'll learn the steps to reconnect you with your body's thin-telligent, optimal nutrition system. Plus we'll look at Wantpower: the inside-out alternative to willpower that equips you to *want* to eat what you currently think you "should." But first, let's take a look at how traditional "outside-in nutrition" can unintentionally steer you wrong.

THE FOUR FATTENING FLAWS
OF TRADITIONAL OUTSIDE-IN NUTRITION

It's very likely that historically your approach towards nutrition has been from the outside in. You take advice on what your body needs based on what "nutritional experts" recommend, consulting a list of foods that *someone else* has deemed to be "good" or "bad." Well, there are four reasons why an outside-in approach to nutritional health hasn't been successful in making people eat more healthfully.

Flaw #1: It assumes your brilliant body is not to be trusted for nutritional guidance.

Traditional outside-in nutrition espouses that your same brilliant physiology—which cranks out 24 million new red blood cells per second, silently orchestrates the fibroblasts and leukocytes to heal a cut, and manages the mind-blowing miracle of creating a new living, breathing human being in your abdomen—is somehow a bumbling blockhead when it comes to selecting premium fuel. The candy wrapper, pastry box, and McDonald's bag debris-strewn aftermath of a painful, demoralizing, out-of-control binge can mistakenly reinforce their assertion. It can be seen as "proof" that your body is *not* to be trusted when it comes to making the best nutritional choices. But as you now know, it is the food rules and restriction—not your body—that is behind those "junk food" cravings.

Flaw #2: Experts can be mistaken. Nutritional recommendations change and can be flat out wrong.

The second drawback of outside-in nutrition is that it can be wrong. There is a long list of medical and nutritional practices that used to be the norm, which now seem incredibly unhealthy— *if not insane.* Leeches, anyone? In George Washington's day, blood-letting was the solution for numerous ailments. So, when the United States' first president had a throat infection, similar to strep throat, the treatment he received involved the draining of massive quantities of his blood before he died. And think about how dangerous cigarette smoking is regarded now. Yet, tobacco smoke was historically thought to be *beneficial* for asthma and tuberculosis. It wasn't until *1970* that the Surgeon General came out with the warning that smoking is actually bad for your health and linked with disease. That wasn't terribly long ago.

The USDA recommendations have changed dramatically over the years. In 1923 they advised people to eat fats that included bacon, lard, and butter. (Nice!) The food pyramid has gone through a number of remodels. Not only can nutrition recommendations evolve—a nice way of saying *"they can be wrong"*—they can be influenced. It's always important when evaluating nutritional recommendations to ask, "Who funded this study?" because the people behind the research or recommendation may have a vested monetary interest in their food product being deemed healthy, and thus recommended.

In addition to the moving target—you have the warring factions. There is no shortage of conflicting nutrition recommendations. One group of experts purport that a diet containing low-fat dairy and lean meats is healthful. Whereas another group of professionals show data suggesting that animal products are harmful for the body and that a plant-based, whole food diet is optimal. It's enough to make your well-intentioned head spin.

How Listening to My Body Cured a Life-Long Skin Ailment in Just Three Weeks

Milk, it does a body good, right? Well, maybe. Unless you're me. Even nutritional information that may be fine for the majority can be wrong for you. I remember as a small child spending countless hours sitting at the kitchen table, protesting having to drink my milk. I loathed milk. I abhorred it. The very thought of it kicked off my gag reflex. I'd have rather eaten a live worm than drink my milk. (I was a dramatic child.) Yet, in her loving attempt to keep me healthy, my well-meaning mom listened to the pediatrician's recommendations and had me drink it. I also had *terrible* eczema. I had the horrific rash on my arms, legs, feet, and face off and on since I was two. This went on for most of my life, until—something happened. Around the same time I started my Hunger Directed Eating journey, I had a particularly nasty flare up on the top of my foot. (Gross, I know. Sorry!) It was so bad. Yet my visits to multiple experts yielded nothing but recommendations for heavy steroids. Well, in addition to being *really* bad for you, steroids make you gain *tons of weight*, so that was completely out of the question for me at that time. So, I just lived with the rash. *Until* I moved into Phase Three of Hunger Directed Eating.

I noticed one morning that, almost miraculously, the recent flare up that had plagued me for over a year was gone. *Vanished.* Puzzled, I wanted to figure it out, "What have I done differently?" And I realized that for the past several months, I had consumed almost no dairy whatsoever. Whenever I would order something that came with cheese—and I used to eat *a ton* of cheese—I would check in with myself and it didn't really sound appealing. So, I would just ask for it without cheese. When I would want something sweet, the thought of ice cream seemed a bit repellant. And because of my research background (and the fact that I'm a nerd), I then launched a little experiment. I ate dairy every day for a week straight. And guess what? *The rash came back.* So now I refer to that rash as my "dairy indicator." Since I've made the conscious decision to not instate any rules around my eating, I still *allow* myself complete, unlimited access to dairy whenever I want it.

But because I've practiced and deeply incorporated Step 5, always checking in to see how the food makes me feel, I almost never want it. Except for when it comes to wood-fired Margherita pizzas, then all bets are off. And luckily, one night of pizza is not enough to elicit the rash. But just about *every* mainstream nutrition book you pick up is going to sing the praises of organic, low-fat dairy, and laud it as a vital part of a healthy diet. So, if I were still listening to that outside-in data, rather than my own body, I would very likely be pumped up with steroids right about now.

Flaw #3: Don't read this section.

Being told *not* to do something practically guarantees that you'll really want to do it. Being told not to eat a certain food, as we've seen, most frequently results in consuming that food—to the point of excess. We've explored in great detail how placing a food off-limits backfires. The moment it becomes restricted, it activates the Non-Hunger Eating chain reaction of Gasping for Food. Which promptly triggers Eating Cuz You Ate. There *is* however an effective technique you can use to influence your eating preferences (which we'll cover in the next section on Wantpower) but as you can guess, relying on external rules isn't it.

Flaw # 4 Knowing what you "shouldn't" eat does absolutely nothing to equip you not to eat it.

Nutritionists mean well. But eating is not an exclusively nutritional issue. There are a host of psychological factors that influence eating behavior that dieticians fail to take into account. The fourth pitfall of outside-in nutrition is probably the most important, because it's where the rubber hits the road. Having a list detailing which foods are good for you and which are bad, does *absolutely nothing* to equip you to follow that list. Here's why—rule-based eating relies exclusively on willpower—and willpower is the ultimate fair-weather friend. Willpower only works, or works its best, when you don't need it. When you're well rested and life is going smoothly, determination can keep you from the candy bowl. But the minute you're tired, stressed, lonely, grumpy, bored, and off your game, you don't have the strength you need to win a brute force battle of the will. So, let's pop the hood and take a closer look at willpower, and the trick to making it work for you when you *really* need it.

WILLPOWER VS. WANTPOWER

Willpower is often used when you're resolutely trying to control your own behavior. It is one way to intentionally manipulate your motivation to get yourself to do what you want to do, like eating nutritious foods. Or conversely, you use it to *not* do something you don't want to do, like eating an entire bag of Chips Ahoy. Willpower is the tool you probably whip out when trying to override your short-term urges in order to obtain your long-term goals. It functions based on a combination of the two basic motivational factors: feelings and time. So, how you feel (pleasure or pain) at a given point in time (now or later). Your behavior will result in you feeling either *good* or *bad*, and you're either going to feel it *now* or *later*. Given this two-dimensional motivation model—influenced by feeling and time—you can only ever be in *one* of *four* motivational states: Want To, Shouldn't, Should, and Won't.

THE FOUR MOTIVATIONAL STATES

	Now	Later
Pleasure	**Want To** Feels good now, good later	**Shouldn't** Feels good now, bad later
Pain	**Should** Feels bad now, good later	**Won't** Feels bad now, bad later

Want To

The first box is for those situations that feel good now *and* feel good later. Playfully tickling your child's belly or going out with your best friend fit into this category. They feel good now, because you're connecting and you're laughing and having fun. And they feel good later, because you're investing in your overall long-term relationships by reinforcing and strengthening your existing close attachments. Experiences in this bucket are what I call Want-To Motivation. It takes *no energy* or *willpower* for me to call one of my best friends. In fact, the real effort comes when I need to *resist* calling them—when I'm scheduled to be doing something else.

Shouldn't

The second box houses experiences that feel seductively good now and feel crummy later. So, eating several donuts for lunch, for example. It feels really good *now* because they taste amazing, and it feels terrible *in an hour* when you're tired, spacey, and bloated. Or, having that second (or third) drink when you're out with your friends. The night's young, you're having a great time, you're caught up in that moment—and it feels fun! But, it feels *miserable* waking up dehydrated, with a pounding headache the next morning. Or, you're at your favorite boutique and you see those adorable shoes, and you absolutely *must* have them, because they will look perfect with that one outfit. And it feels exhilarating to buy them. *Now.* You feel the adrenaline surge as they put the box in the glossy bag, and you prance out the door with them. But, it feels *lousy* later when you open your credit card bill, heart nervously racing, as you spiral into a financial freak out. The experiences in this category are the Shouldn'ts. Unlike Want-To, which is a pure motivational state—feels good now, feels good later—the Shouldn't is a conflicted emotional state. It feels great when you're doing it, but terrible on the back end.

Should

Similarly, the third box contains the second conflicted state, Should. Shoulds are the things that feel really *hard* now, but they feel *amazing* later, once you finish them. Things like cleaning your bathroom— not that fun, or glamorous. But when you're done and are met with sparkling floors and fixtures, accented by the smell of freshly laundered, fluffy towels, it feels fabulous! Another example is getting up and going for a walk. You feel tired and stressed and it feels like more effort than you can muster to unglue yourself from the couch and get out for a quick walk. But once you've done it, your heart's beating, your juices are flowing, you feel vibrant, energetic—alive. The Shoulds feel really tough in the now, when you're doing them or getting started, but they feel really good later, and you're always very glad you did them. Again, this is a conflicted motivational state. The negative is on the front end, it feels tough when you're doing it, or getting started—and the pleasure comes at the back end.

Won't

The last of the four motivational states are things that feel terrible now and they feel terrible later—the Won'ts. These are things you just simply won't do, like munching on dryer lint. It takes not one ounce of willpower. You're just *not going to do it*. There's no conflict. Like touching a hot stove, it feels terrible now when your hand is getting burned, and it feels terrible later, when your finger starts to blister up.

PURE AND CONFLICTING MOTIVATIONAL STATES

When feeling states (pleasure and pain) are constant over time (you feel good or bad now *and* later)—as in the case of Want To's and Won'ts—you are in a *pure motivational state*. When the feeling changes with time, as with Shoulds and Shouldn'ts, you are in a *conflicted motivational state*. Pure states require no flexing of your will. Conflicting states, as the name suggests, are fraught with… well, with conflict. They require strong-arming for one side to win. When behaviors fall into the two *pure* motivational categories (Want To and Won't) they require not one extra ounce of mental energy. No willpower. They simply run on autopilot. Even when you're tired, bored, lonely, stressed, or anxious, it takes no determination or will to *not* chew a piece of broken glass. Right? You're just not going to do it. But it is the conflicting motivational states (Should and Shouldn't), on the other hand, that set you up for a rough ride from the start. Unless you're in prime, well-rested, highly motivated form, you're going to lose the battle of the will. Because managing your behavior by an iron will—rather than autopilot—is a constant, energy-draining source of conflict and tension. You're in an unending arm wrestle between "Do it!" and "Don't do it!" The instant you're weakened, distracted, or slightly off your game, your resolve caves in the direction of whatever is the least painful, and most pleasurable, in that moment. So, you *won't* be flossing your teeth, and you *will* be sitting in front of the TV eating cheesecake.

WANTPOWER: HOW TO WANT TO EAT WHAT IS ACTUALLY GOOD FOR YOU

Step 5 of Hunger Directed Eating, *Check In to See How the Food Makes You Feel* uses your body's feedback about how certain foods actually work for (or against) you to transform the Shoulds into Want To's and the Shouldn'ts into Wont's. For example, prior to mastering Step 5, I knew that I *shouldn't* eat cupcakes and pastries for lunch. The problem was, this Shouldn't was based on external data—my diet-based belief that sweets were "fattening" and "bad" for me. Yet cakes and pastries were my kryptonite. They would call to me from the world-class San Francisco bakery across the street from my office. I was a serious bakeshop junkie.

But when I released the brake and let myself have them whenever I wanted them, and (*importantly*) paired that with Step 5 of checking in to see how they felt in my body—something transformational happened. Previously when I would eat sweets on my lunch break—donuts, brownies, cookies, whatever—I would be consumed with the frenzied food chatter swirling around in my head. (You might be familiar with this.) I was so busy beating myself up, feeling guilty, or completely checking out—so I could mute the Eat/Don't Eat battle being waged in my head—that I was completely detached from my body. With all that craziness going on upstairs, I didn't have the mental space to stop and actually observe or register how the food *physically* made me feel.

My work has always been very analytical. At that time I was a senior database architect for the largest decisions support database in the U.S., which *inconveniently* required that I actually be cognitively present while I worked. Well, when I first started playing around with Step 5 (checking in with my body to see how *it* felt about what I just ate) I—for the first time *ever*—noticed and made the connection between the cherry cheese danish I had at lunch, and the brain fog that struck me forty minutes later, as I sat staring at my computer. The neurons would fire in my brain and it was like that phenomenon where you walk into a room and you think to yourself, *I know I came in here for something, but I can't remember what it was...* My brain would be in that fuzzy unproductive state for the rest of the afternoon. When I started to take note of how my *body* was running on pastry fuel, I realized that I felt tired, grumpy, and completely unable to concentrate. Simply *noticing* this discomfort powerfully changed the motivational pull I had created around starchy sweets from Shouldn't to

Won't. For the first time *ever*, this feedback enabled me to build a bridge between how I was feeling physically (Step 5)—and what I really, really wanted to eat (Step 2). So, the next day at lunch, when I had *full permission* to eat a cherry cheese danish again, I looked at it in the glass case and I remembered how terrible I felt the day before. And, from the inside out, I *genuinely wanted* something different—because I wanted to avoid the pain of feeling tired, grumpy, and fuzzy-headed.

So my old conflicting Shouldn't, "I *shouldn't* eat pastries for lunch, even though I really, really want to," turned into a Want To, or Won't (depending on how you look at it). I *want* to eat something that is better fuel, or I *won't* eat something that is going to make me feel that terrible again—early in the day. I'll still eat pastry-type sweets at night, because quite frankly, I don't care if I feel dumb or tired then. But seriously, now you could not *pay* me to ruin my whole day's productivity by eating a donut in the middle of the afternoon.

You see, before using Step 5 to check in with how the food made me feel, things played out in a pretty predictable fashion. When I looked at a brownie or cream puff in the glass bakery case, I would think, "I shouldn't have it, because it's *bad* for me"—and then I'd get swept into the whole *"eat it, don't eat it,"* debate. Well, being "bad for me" is a vague, intangible concept, hardly a match for the *very real* recollection of how delicious the thick, rich, nutty, fudgy brownie tastes. And often, I ended up giving in and going for the (seemingly) pleasurable treat. But now—after checking in—I have the very *concrete, tangible* memory of feeling lethargic, grumpy, and slightly depressed anchored to the experience in my body after I ate the previously revered sweet. So, the next time that I was presented with this food, it automatically started migrating from a *Shouldn't* to a *"Won't."* Which is a pure motivational state—and moves it into the *effortless* category. So you'll be free to bypass the brownie at lunch without an ounce of willpower.

FROM DONUTS AND DORITOS TO INSIDE-OUT OPTIMUM NUTRITION

There are two different ways you can accelerate your journey through the less-than-nutrient-rich initial phase of reintroducing restricted foods: *releasing the food brake*, and *checking in to see how the food makes you feel*. These two tricks will help you hightail it through Donuts and Doritos and arrive in the lush, verdant land of healthy eating. You'll learn how to make choices from the inside out, driven by what your body—not your poor, diet-deprived (and sometimes depraved!) mind—desires for optimum fuel.

1. Release the brake (Should and Shouldn't)

Only *partially* reintroducing forbidden foods is like trying to drive your car with the parking brake on. You're going to get to your destination much more slowly, and with much more resistance. As long as you're restricting, your food choices are reactions to deprivation, rather than responses to your body's fuel and nutrient needs. If you leave the food brake on, even a little bit—allowing yourself to eat certain foods but not others—you are more likely to struggle with an exaggerated drive to eat whatever is still banned.

The paradox of inside-out nutrition is that it is by allowing yourself to eat cake and cookies, you will end up eating far more nutrient-rich foods in the long run. It makes (counterintuitive) sense then, that releasing the brake is an essential first step to being able to respond to what your body needs—without the rebellious chatter of Gasping. Letting yourself eat the old kryptonite Foods can be incredibly scary. If your past has been painfully tyrannized by overeating, then reintroducing some of these foods can feel *really intimidating*. So, I encourage you to be really nice to yourself during this process. If it doesn't feel safe to release it all at once, or all in one month, or even all in six months, that is *perfectly all right*. Take it at the exact speed that feels safe.

2. Check in to see how the food makes you feel (Want To and Won't)

The second practice that is going to catapult you through Donuts and Doritos into pure Hunger Directed Eating is Step 5, which is the simple but brilliant practice of checking in and noticing how the food you last ate serves you. So, how do you do it? Well, at a high level, you do Step 5 by simply checking in with yourself thirty minutes, an hour, three hours, and again up to five hours after you've eaten. Rate how you're feeling on the following variables: energy, hunger, mood, concentration, as well as other systemic factors like digestion. The trick is to actually remember to do it. Setting an alarm on your phone to remind you to check in is really useful at the beginning. Then you just take a deep breath; get out of your head and into your body and check in. You can do this by focusing on the following sensations.

A. Assess your hunger

How effectively did what you last ate satisfy your hunger? Does it keep you going with a steady, solid, stable three on the hunger scale? Are you able to go for three, four, or five hours comfortably sustained? You're not really hungry, you're not excessively full, you're just moving forward in that great, efficiently fueled state. Which then slowly, moderately, politely tapers down hours later and you are gently motivated to start thinking about eating again. You'll probably (and very rationally) be highly motivated to *re-create* that evenly sustained experience. You can do this simply by anchoring back that pleasantly sustained sensation to whatever it was that you ate. It's in this way that you start to really figure out (for yourself) what works best for *your* body. I like to call it experiential, or hands-on, inside-out nutrition. Like many people, I had always heard from the outside in that you should eat protein with every meal. However, it was a list, it was a rule—I didn't do it. But once I started using Step 5 and checking in with myself, I noticed *I felt great* when I ate protein. My hunger wouldn't return for something like five hours. And when it did, it would be that very gentle sensation, tapering off into an easy, polite hunger. So now, protein is in the pure motivational state of, "I want to eat it with every meal," because I *love* how it makes me feel.

I am in no way saying that the answer to being slim and feeling great is to eat protein with every meal. Again, if you were to listen to me saying that and apply it to your life, it would be an outside-in rule. I look at my best girlfriend, who is a size zero, naturally thin eater, and she eats *very differently* than how I eat. She feels much better when she has more fat and carbohydrate with each of her meals. That's what keeps *her* optimally performing, because her body doesn't react the same way as mine. This single method enables you to comfortably reach your naturally thin body weight eating what is *uniquely* right for *you*.

FAKE PHYSIOLOGICAL HUNGER:
THE BLOOD-SUGAR CRASH

On the other side of the hunger equation you might notice that thirty minutes after eating certain foods, you will have the *bottom-drop-out-hunger*. This is the blood sugar equivalent of the roller coaster that takes you up, up, up. And your blood sugar, like the roller coaster car, moves forward over the edge, you hear a couple clicks, and then—whoosh—the bottom drops out and you free fall for 80 stories.

Have you ever eaten your body weight in pancakes and syrup, and been *baffled* that you were starving and craving sugar like a fiend just 40 minutes later? Well, remember when we talked about the differences between physical hunger and counterfeit hunger (Step 1)? By practicing Step 5, I discovered that there is a third type of hunger—fake physiological hunger—also affectionately known as the "blood sugar binge and blues." When I ate a meal consisting of simple carbohydrates, tons of sugar, and *very little* protein or fiber (something like pancakes with syrup), I would consume enough fuel, calorically speaking, to launch me through at least half of the day. Yet never fail, 45 minutes after eating, the bottom would drop out and I would be ravenous. I felt tired, spacey, grumpy, a little sad—and all I wanted in the world was a box of donuts (or two). And I was perplexed about how I could possibly be so hungry again so soon. Eventually I figured out that I had triggered *fake physiological hunger*, which is a blood sugar response.

I call it *fake* physiological hunger because it is a true (powerful) physiological response but it is fake in that your body doesn't truly need more fuel. By consuming a high volume of simple carbohydrate, low protein, and low fiber, you cause your blood sugar to spike. Your body, in its infinite wisdom, preserves your life by releasing insulin to lower your elevated blood sugar. You see, low blood sugar in its normal scenario (when you *haven't* flooded your system with simple sugars) is usually the sign that your body needs more fuel. So naturally it triggers—you guessed it—*hunger*. And not just any hunger.

You experience a very intense, *Must Eat Now* urgency that is a true physiological response—because the insulin has caused your blood sugar to crash. This sets you up for very powerful cravings, because your body's life-preserving response is getting you to take the actions necessary to raise your blood sugar. That action being diving into a box of donuts. Talk about a vicious cycle! Once you experience one of these fake physiological hungers—and how terrible you feel from riding the blood sugar roller coaster—from the inside, you won't find these foods *quite so attractive* anymore. And your mind will begin to anchor this particular food to the negative sugar-craving rollercoaster it creates.

B. Measure your energy, concentration, and mood

Are you feeling alert, ready to go after your last meal—your body's surging with clean, focused, resourceful energy? Or are you feeling sluggish, and the mere thought of getting up out of your chair and walking *all the way* over to the printer feels like way more physical exertion than you can possibly handle? How's your concentration? (This was *huge* for me.) Are you feeling crisp, sharp, and alert, thoroughly able to bring your full intellect to the task at hand? Or are you finding it difficult to concentrate, and having that—walk into a room but can't remember what you came in there for—fuzzy brain feeling? Finally, how is your mood? (This one was also huge for me—*and* everyone else around me!) Are you optimistic and upbeat with that spring in your step? Are you calm, centered, and peaceful? Or, are you kind of sad, unmotivated and depressed?

Sugars, carbohydrates, and proteins really do act like drugs in your body and have a profound influence on your *energy*, your *concentration*, and your *mood*. One of my friends knows that whenever I eat sugary foods in the middle of the day, I take an emotional nosedive. We were at a posh waterfront café looking at the pastry case, when I said, "Oh, wow that cinnamon roll looks really good." Without missing a beat, he turned to me and fired back, "No way, if you order that you're going to be crying on my shoulder in an hour."

C. Examine your digestion, hormonal balance, etc. How are you overall?

And the third thing to consider are the more systemic factors. How is your digestion? What about your skin? How about your female cycle? These variables can take a bit more time to iden-tify and link to specific foods. But just as ditching dairy had a profound impact on my skin irritation, I've had some *really sig-nificant* discoveries about how certain foods impact my feminine cycle. (I could write a whole other book on that one!) I've gone from being a bloated, depressed wreck for 14 consecutive days, to having mostly uneventful, easy cycles simply by fine-tuning what I eat from the inside out. I get emails from people all over the world about how eating this way has yielded benefits far beyond effortless(ish) weight loss. One accomplished personal trainer wrote in excitement to share that in under three months of Hunger Directed Eating, she *completely eliminated* the acne that had plagued her for years.

Your body really is brilliant! So go ahead, set your alarm, and without judgment or preconceived, external, nutritional guidelines, truly check in at various points after your meals to see what it has to say about what you last ate. A lot of people like to keep a notepad or a file on their phone where they can just jot down a rating of their hunger stability, one to five. Five being super stable, one being bottom-drop-out hunger. Rate your energy level, mood, concentration—again, one being lousy and five being optimal. And finally, jot down notes on some longer-reaching systemic responses that you're noticing, like your complexion, digestion, etc. You will finally enjoy lasting healthful leanness as you build the bridge between eating whatever it is you really, *really* want (Step 2), and noticing *how* your body *feels* in response to what you've eaten (Step 5). Soon, there will be *no separation between* what you truly desire, from the inside out, and the foods that optimally fuel your body.

chapter nine

MEASURING YOUR SLIM SUCCESS

With Your Sanity
& Without the Scale

THE DIETER AND THE SCALE:
THE ULTIMATE LOVE-HATE RELATIONSHIP

There is no more intense love-hate relationship than that between a dieter and her scale. That little number has the power to make or break your mood, your day, or your entire week. It is a tyrant. A cruel dictator. A low number and you are elated, powerful—on top of your game. A higher number and you shrivel into frustration, self-directed rage, and despair. The rituals we create around weighing ourselves are just about as nutty as Eating Cuz You Ate. We give the scale supreme power over our lives yet at the same time we *completely distrust it*, as evidenced by the dieter's morning scale dance. You might be familiar with this one. It's first thing in the morning, you're stark naked (and already visited the toilet), you hold your breath and step onto the square fortuneteller with the apprehension of someone stepping into a freezing pool. You step off the scale and take a moment to register the all-powerful number that was staring up at you. Then *what* do you do next? Well you get right back on to see if the number's the same—*of course*. Right? No other single product in our home can bring out our OCD tendencies the way a scale can. It often becomes a highly ritualized practice. You weigh yourself at the *same* exact time every day, wearing the *same* exact thing (which is usually nothing), at the *same* exact place. These behaviors themselves are a tip-off showing us how *little* faith we have in this four-sided piece of metal that we let run our lives. With all this obsession around the scale, it's not surprising that a question I get asked a lot by both clients and Thin TV viewers is: "How often should I weigh myself?" My answer: Never. Here's why.

THE FIVE REASONS THE SCALE ISN'T THE BEST WAY TO TRACK YOUR PROGRESS

The desire to track and measure your slimming progress is an incredibly normal and constructive pursuit. The ability to concretely quantify your success is a valid human need—however, the scale is *not* the ideal tool for the job. There are five key reasons why the scale is a flawed apparatus for tracking your success.

1. Your weight fluctuates hourly for reasons other than fat gain or loss.

What you've been eating, your hydration level, whether you gave the salt a shake, and the time of day (or *month!*) are just a handful of the countless factors that can significantly distort the number that appears on the scale. The scale is a profoundly unreliable day-to-day measure of your overall thinness progress, because your weight can fluctuate several pounds in a single 24-hour cycle. The scale can only ever tell you one thing—what your body (and anything and everything temporarily in it) weighs at that precise moment. As I noted above, this number vacillates wildly based on a large number of variables, only *one* of which is your actual fat content. Chug a bottle of water, your weight goes up. Let yourself get dehydrated, it goes down. Dehydration is harmful to your body, yet the scale presents that unhealthy water loss as (desired) weight loss "success" when you hop on and you're four (water) pounds lighter. Similarly, (but in the *other* direction) the scale rockets skyward if your digestion is backed up or you're retaining water—only to sink right back down after things get moving. And your weight will tend to creep up due to hormonal shifts right before your period. Which is a bit of a sick joke, because that is *the worst* time to be dealt a fake pound or two!

2. The scale doesn't measure your *real* goal—fat loss.

Your body weight is made up of three main components: lean body mass (muscles, organs, and bones), fat, and water. When you lose weight you obviously want to lose fat, not muscle or your spleen. Right? Well, when you use body weight (as opposed to other measures) to gauge your success, the scale can be incredibly deceptive. What happens if we take a closer look at these numbers? Let's say that while Lauren was practicing Hunger Directed Eating she lost four pounds in week one, in week two she lost two pounds, and in week three her weight stayed the same—according to the scale. It can be understandably frustrating (if not maddening) to be diligently eating when you're hungry and stopping when you're full all week just as you did the previous ones and not lose a single pound. But with a different, more accurate, measurement device, this same scenario could be viewed *very* differently. Measuring body composition (the ratio of fat, water, and lean mass) tells us a completely different story. Lauren started out at 30% body fat. While looking at actual changes in her body fat percentage, it turns out that in week one her total fat mass was 29.5% of her body weight (a half a percent loss), in week two it was 28.5% (a one percent loss) and in week three it was 26.5% (a two percent loss!). So in week three, when her body weight was at a standstill with the scale indicating that she made *no* progress, it was actually the week she made the *most* progress. She lost the most fat—which was her goal. I'm not recommending that you use body composition testing to replace the scale (you'll soon learn what I *do* recommend using), I'm simply illustrating how misleading the scale is, and how it can misrepresent real progress. This is insidious because one of the main reasons for tracking your progress is to identify what you're doing that *is* working to move you closer to your goal—so you can repeat it. If during the week that you're actually making the *most significant* advancement towards your desired outcome you're getting *incorrect* feedback, you're at a much higher risk of chucking (or second-guessing) the successful techniques that will keep you moving forward.

3. Scale fluctuations can have motivationally devastating effects.

Have you ever had one of those days where you wake up feeling really lean, your stomach's flat—you just *know* you've lost weight! So you excitedly rush to weigh yourself. You step on the scale and wait with giddy anticipation as the magic number registers… and you can't believe your eyes. You're three and a half pounds—*up*. What? How is that possible?! Your great mood instantly crash-lands onto the bathroom floor. Your thoughts spiral down into an abyss. *All* that work you did. *All* that effort. And for *what*? Failure!! Intense feelings of hopelessness and futility sweep over you. Just moments before you were eager, optimistic, successful. *Now*—you're devastated, unmotivated, and feeling utterly power-less. "What's the use?" you resignedly ask yourself… as you turn around and head to the kitchen, seeking out a snack to soothe your growing distress and numb your mounting pain.

We've just seen the scads of variables that can affect the num-ber on the scale: You could very well have indeed lost fat, but may have simply been retaining water. Or, maybe you could have actually gained that weight. But either way, the act of step-ping on the scale and receiving a different (higher) number than you anticipated can have a devastating impact on your mood. Which can then lead to… (wait for it) *overeating*.

4. Studies show frequent self-weighing leads to binge eating.

A recent University of Minnesota study found that frequent self-weighing "predicted a higher frequency of binge eating and unhealthy weight control behaviors." By this point, data like that probably doesn't come as a big shocker. If weigh-ins are a source of immense frustration, disappointment, and emotional distress, it makes perfect sense that they would add fuel to the throw-in-the-towel-all-or-nothing-binge-eating fire.

My Crazy Scale Story

Placing such monumental importance on *exactly* what the scale says—then having that number bob up and down depending on a single glass of water—can literally drive you crazy. And the "scale insanity" doesn't only apply to the number rising, even when you *are* losing weight, not losing *as much as you anticipated* can cause a treacherous tailspin. Sad, but true. If your relationship with food and the scale has been anywhere near as chaotic as mine used to be, you can probably relate to the story of the last time I weighed myself (*years* ago). I was on my last formal diet ever, a very popular one where you purchased their prepared food and weighed in every week. For three long, grueling weeks I ate only their cardboard frozen meals in the *exact* quantities that I was supposed to—not a *single* morsel of anything else. And each week I lost two pounds. I was a shining example of the truly dedicated dieter. I exercised religiously (solely to burn calories) and faithfully ate according to the program's guidelines—down to the *exact* last allotted calorie. Every. Single. Day. But *this* week, week four, was special. Because if I lost the two pounds that I had been consistently losing, I would break into the newer, *lower*, ten-pound range. And all you professional dieters out there know that the two pounds at the top or middle of a ten-pound weight range are *entirely* different than the two pounds that take you down—to that newer, lighter, thinner category. Then, you're in a *whole new lower decile.* Totally different.

So, I had been painstakingly on target with my eating and I was convinced that the coveted next lower range was going to be mine. I eagerly arrived at the center wearing my slip-off shoes and the same dress I wore the week before (for consistency, *naturally*), and cheerfully chatted with the woman who was going to weigh me. Then, I got on the scale. And I had lost… 1.5 pounds. (What?!) My heart plummeted in my chest. NO WAY. Instead of being down in that new, lighter, thinner, "better" range, there I was. *Still in the same decile.* (Albeit at the *very* bottom, just a *half* a pound away from where I had thought I would be). But it didn't matter (or even register) that I was close. *I hadn't made it.* That was it—I came completely unhinged. I could feel the hot tears begin to well up in my eyes. With all the composure I could muster I put on my shoes, grabbed my purse, and—bolted. I had deprived myself of even a single bite of pleasurable food for *four weeks.* I orchestrated each hour of each day around this blasted diet. I even brought my stupid frozen cardboard pizza to my girlfriend's house for our lunch date. I had clung on to that number all week to get me through. And all the exercise and deprivation didn't deliver. I snapped. I walked directly out the door, got into my car and drove straight to the Taco Bell drive thru across the parking lot. I was crestfallen, demoralized… and supremely fed up. I figured, "What the heck, I did absolutely *everything* right and I still didn't get down to that lower weight range." So I sat in my car angrily, dejectedly, ravenously eating my burrito, tostada, and funky (gross) cinnamon crisp things. Then I continued on, eating my way through the rest of the day. And that was the last time I ever weighed myself.

Of course, this sounds completely illogical (okay, *insane)* to the casual reader. But I know that for those of you who have been sucked into that scale-based insanity, you can relate to the sinkhole an unfavorable scale reading can create. That weigh-in hit on *so many years* of futility. It smacked of the herculean effort I consistently (obsessively) put out trying to lose weight. And yet, no matter *how much* I dieted I wasn't making real, sustainable, lasting progress toward my goal. I don't ever even think of that scale episode anymore, so recalling it now brings up a surge of emotions. Mostly gratitude that I have blown the roof off of what I thought my goal was, and that I now live in my naturally thin body eating *whatever* I want, with the peace, comfort, and certainty that it will be mine—*forever*. The other burst of emotion that arises is a fierce determination to spread this message of freedom to absolutely *anyone* who currently hurts about food and their weight. It is my goal to provide you with a step-by-step roadmap out of *"diet hell."* So you too can make peace with food, joyfully relax into your naturally thin body, and get on with your fabulous life.

5. Naturally thin people don't regularly weigh themselves.

This entire thin-telligence approach is based on resolving eating issues at the root level, and modeling naturally thin eaters' behavior. So, when trying to make my decision about what I wanted to do with the scale I interviewed all the naturally thin eaters that I knew. (Okay, all the naturally thin eaters that I knew well enough to probe them about their weighing habits.) I had done this kind of survey on various topics throughout my exploration, but the scale was the one topic where (astonishingly) *every single* naturally thin eater that I queried had the *exact* same answer.

First, when I asked each of them how often they weighed themselves, they consistently replied, "Oh, probably like twice a year." And it would always be at the doctor's office, or a spa, or a fancy hotel that had a scale in the bathroom—never at home. Bewildered, I asked the follow-up question, "Then how do you gauge or keep track of your weight?" And across the board, each naturally thin eater said the *same* thing, "Well, I can just tell by how my jeans fit." Every. Single. One. So, modeling these experts, I took this brilliant gem of information and applied it to creating my positive-progress-tracker scale alternative.

HOW TO TRACK YOUR THIN-PROGRESS WITHOUT SHOOTING YOURSELF IN THE FOOT

Wanting feedback on your progress is a valid human need. It is also a very effective way to reach a goal. But only if the measurement tool *itself* doesn't sabotage your success. The fact that the scale doesn't measure the right thing (fat loss) *and* is highly unreliable (fluctuating hourly) renders it an extraordinarily poor choice when it comes to accurately monitoring your slimming success. So, if the scale has the tendency to land you in the pit of despair—or the drive-thru—perhaps it's time to mix it up. I invite you to play around with swapping it out, and for the next month or two try tracking your thin-progress just like the pros (naturally thin eaters) do—by monitoring how your clothes fit.

The Skinny Jean (or Slim Skirt) Scale

Simply pick a skirt, a pair of jeans or a dress that is snug and use it to track your success. You can use it in the exact same way that you use the scale. Swapping the scale for a designated clothing item has had a very liberating, binge-stopping, peace-of-mind-giving impact for many of my clients. They are amazed at how well it can satisfy that need to "check in" and see real progress *without* causing the (day-ruining) angst of the scale.

I live in skirts—so I went with a particular navy blue pencil skirt. It was pretty tight... okay (full disclosure), it was *so* tight that I couldn't zip it all the way up, and the strain on the material made it pucker to such an extent that it created horizontal ocean-like waves across the front of my thighs. It was not fit to be worn in public. But for these purposes it was—*perfect*. So I made it my Slim Skirt Scale. Any time I was seeking feedback about my thinning progress, I would try on the skirt and monitor changes in how it fit. You know those mornings where you wake up and want to check in: *How am I doing? I'm feeling leaner! Did I move forward?* That's when I would try on the skirt. In the beginning (when my thinking was still painfully chaotic) on some days I would try it on a couple of times—just like I would have weighed myself back in my "psycho scale days."

Once your Slim Scale gets too big—if you are not yet at your naturally thin body weight—you simply pick (or buy) another item of clothing that is slightly snug. It is best to use something only a few sizes too small so you can experience the mastery of moving on to another item. I can't adequately express to you in words the feelings of self-efficacy I had when that same skirt reclaimed its status of not being fit for public, but this time... because it was too big and it wouldn't stay up! For *years* I kept that skirt as a cherished (tangible) reminder of how far I had come.

So, to conclude, the Skirt or Skinny Jeans Slim Scale gives you the measurement, feedback, and objective external validation you need to track that you *are* in fact moving in the right direction. But, it does it in a gentler way, as opposed to an exact number, where just half a pound can ruin your whole day. (Or longer.) Another great aspect of the Clothes Scale is that you'll once again have the tangible experience of the item fitting in such a way that it won't be appropriate to be worn in public—but this time it will be because it is *way too big*! So, what will *you* pick to be your Slim Scale?

chapter ten

EXERCISE: LOVE IT OR LEAVE IT

It's Not Required—But
It Will Lift Your Bum & Your Mood

ARE YOU SAYING I DON'T HAVE TO EXERCISE?

Think about the naturally thin eaters you know. Their weight seems to stay mind-bogglingly consistent over time—independent of whether they have a gym membership. Right? When trying to lose weight, dieters often use exercise to "cheat the system" by manipulating the calories-in vs. calories-out ratio. So, where does exercise fit into this new approach to lasting leanness? Let me be clear. To get and stay thin, exercise is *not* required.

Okay, at this point you're probably thinking, "Wait a minute, is she really telling me that I can get thin while eating whatever I want (even chocolate) and I don't have to force myself to exercise?" Yes, I am. From a purely biological perspective your body's thin-telligence system will easily get you to and keep you at your naturally lean weight through Hunger Directed Eating.

Exercise is not required. Just look at all of your naturally thin friends who are consistently slim yet they aren't slaves to the gym. However, the goal of this chapter isn't to encourage you to not exercise—it's to examine your relationship with it. So that, just like with food, exercise can go back to its rightful place in your life. Where it serves you, not the other way around.

Studies show that when approached from a diet-logic mindset working out can boomerang into (*you guessed it*) overeating. Dieting can also turn exercise into a socially accepted form of bulimia, used to purge excess calories consumed, or to pave the way to overeat later by creating a calorie deficit beforehand. This is a painful, exhausting, unnecessary relationship. We are going to examine the common *mis*perceptions about the role of exercise in weight loss that don't support your efforts—or stand up against the data. You'll discover how to build a relationship with exercise where you can ditch the drama and enjoy its many benefits. (Plus we'll uncover the surprising way exercise *can* spare you thousands of calories.)

THE FIVE REASONS WHY EXERCISE ISN'T THE SHORTCUT TO SLIM

Exercise yields sensational unparalleled life- and mood-enhancing benefits—but sustained weight loss is *not* one of them. Let's explore the five reasons why exercise isn't your best bet for getting and staying thin.

Reason #1: Exercise Relies on Willpower

Okay, there is probably no more deluded logic than those late night "open-fridge negotiations." It's ten-thirty at night, you've already had two bowls of chocolate peanut butter cup ice cream, and you're standing with the freezer door open, debating a third. That's when the chatter starts up. *Eat it!* Don't eat it! It's clear that you're not hungry. You know you'll feel disappointed (and bloated) if you eat it. But you *really* want it. Then you have a light bulb moment, "I've got it! I'll go ahead eat it now and *tomorrow* I'll be really good." As if somehow magically tomorrow morning you'll have access to the vast supply of willpower that is currently eluding you. (I think we've all fallen for this one at least once or twice.) If willpower isn't there for you on the front end of the agreement to fortify you against the Non-Hunger Eating, what makes you trust it will be there tomorrow morning for a six a.m. post-ice-cream run? When the alarm blares indicating that it's time to work off your indulgence—and you're tired, nestled in your warm bed—it will be very tempting to hit the snooze button, *not* the pavement.

If you're *not* exercising for the love of it, but as a form of calorie-penance, working out slips from the pure motivation *Want To* category—to the conflicted motivation category of *Should*. This means that whenever you're tired, stressed, or otherwise off of your game, you probably *won't* be exercising. And if being lean depends on you burning those calories—you're going to be up a creek. Without a paddle.

Reason #2: Exercise Is Not Sustainable in All Situations

If you are relying on exercise to keep your caloric deficit intact, you're putting yourself at high risk of packing on the pounds when situations arise where working out isn't feasible. Hunger Directed Eating enables complete freedom with food, allowing you to get and stay thin in *any* situation—whether you simply have a busy week scheduled, relatives in town, a cold, or (heaven forbid!) a broken leg.

Reason #3: It's Not How Naturally Thin People Get and Stay Thin

Naturally thin people do not rely on exercise to be lean. Some of them love riding bikes, practicing yoga, or running (while others don't even *own* gym shoes), but their leanness is in no way *dependent* on maintaining these activities. If they stop working out for a while, for whatever reason, their weight does not noticeably fluctuate. You won't hear them complaining that their jeans are feeling tight. Though you *may* hear them lamenting not being physical—but only because of how good they feel when they exercise. Since they are eating according to hunger and fullness—when they don't exercise, their body's thin-telligence automatically adjusts their caloric needs, and communicates the updates (real-time) through their appetite mechanism. No muss, no fuss.

So not only is exercise not *required* for you to get and stay thin when you are eating between hunger and fullness—it won't make you lose weight any faster. Your body knows exactly how much fuel you need. If you run for ten miles you will need more fuel than if you were just watching a movie on the couch. Therefore when you work out, you will simply be hungry more often than if you didn't. It is only if you exercise then *ignore* the corresponding increased hunger signals your body sends that you would create an exercise-induced calorie deficit. And we've already seen the mess that overriding your body's thin-telligence creates.

Reason #4: Exercise Is Insanely Inefficient

Using exercise as a way to shift the calories-in vs. calories-out ratio is supremely inefficient when you consider the amount of time it takes to eat something versus the time it takes to work it off. Let's do the math. Say you eat a cheeseburger with fries. It will take you *five* to *six* hours of walking to burn it off. If you throw in a milkshake (or a margarita) you're looking at another three to four hours of walking. So if you're relying on exercise to compensate for your calories, *clearly* you'll need to quit your job because you're already up to *ten hours* of walking and we haven't even made it through lunch! I used calorically dense foods in this example but even a banana takes just under an hour of walking to burn off. So even if you do have the willpower when facing the treadmill that eluded you when you were facing the cheesecake, you would still spend the majority of your waking hours working off your food. And that is *not* freedom.

But doesn't muscle burn more fat? The surprising truth.

How many extra calories do you think you could eat each day if you replaced ten pounds of fat with ten pounds of muscle? You always hear that muscle burns more calories than fat. Which is true, but the difference is *egregiously* exaggerated. Research published in the *Journal of Obesity* calculated that one pound of muscle burns *six* calories per day. Fat on the other hand burns *two* calories a day. So a pound of muscle burns four more calories per day than a pound of fat. But hold on before you race to cash those calories in on cream puffs. Let's say you lost ten pounds of body fat and replaced it with muscle—that's the equivalent to 40 cubes of butter—a *huge* accomplishment. But when you add it up, converting those ten one pound boxes of butter from your belly and thighs to muscle only burns *forty* extra calories per day. Total. So those ten pounds of muscle afford you a whopping extra tea-spoon (*not tablespoon!*) of olive oil. Hardly the get-out-of-calories-free card that diet-lore advertises it to be.

Reason #5: Oh Yeah, It Doesn't Work

Exercise will irrefutably make you happier, healthier, and more cognitively flexible—however, it *won't* make you thin. The Chair of Diabetes and Metabolism at Louisiana State University and prominent exercise researcher, Eric Ravussin boldly summarizes it like this, "In general, for weight loss, exercise is pretty use-less." (This is the Chair of Diabetes and Metabolism and a lead-ing exercise analyst!) In a 2009 *Time Magazine* article titled *Why Exercise Won't Make You Thin*, he explains, "Many recent studies have found that exercise isn't as important in helping people lose weight as you hear so regularly."

EXERCISE DOES NOT WORK FOR SUSTAINED WEIGHT LOSS.

Using exercise to tweak your body's calories-in vs. calo-ries-burned ratio in order to lose weight seems perfectly reason-able, on paper. Just like manipulating food intake with dieting, but in this case instead of eating fewer calories than you burn, you'll just exercise the pounds away. Right? You'll simply burn more calories than you eat and—presto, weight loss! But again (like when you restrict food) this logic fails to take into account the psychological response (backlash) that this cardio-based method produces. Just like the Gasping response, exercising from this deprivation mindset has the exact *opposite* effect than intended—it leads to overeating.

One of Ravussin's colleagues conducted a study to empirically measure the impact of exercise on weight loss. He divided 464 obese women into four groups. One group was asked not to exercise, while the other three groups worked with a personal trainer for six months, each exercising for different amounts of time (ranging from 1-3 hours). And get this: The results showed that there was NO significant difference in fat loss between the women sweating it out with a trainer *for six months* and those that didn't lace up a single gym shoe. In fact, some of the women in the exercise group even gained weight over the course of the study—some over ten pounds.

Not only did the weight-loss-focused fitness regime lead to the women in the exercise groups *eating more* food in general during the study, they specifically ate more "junk food." The women reported eating more donuts, chips, and candy than they did before the study. Overeating in response to weight-loss-motivated exercising is known as The Boomerang Effect. As you know, when we shift our calories-in by restricting food we end up Gasping for Food. Well, it turns out that when we manipulate the calories-out in order to lose weight by exercising (rather than exercising for the love of it) we end up boomeranging into a binge as well. When interviewed, the women explained that they ate more of the indulgent foods during the experiment because they felt like they needed a reward. The women also explained they thought they could "cheat" without it impacting their weight because they had worked out. Well, if you're banking on those thirty minutes in spin class to make up for the three extra éclairs you ate last night—it's sadly just not going to cut it.

HOW BREAKING UP WITH WORKING OUT SPARKED MY LOVE AFFAIR WITH EXERCISE

People frequently write in and ask if I exercised years ago back when I lost the weight. And the answer is… No. (*Shock. Disbelief.*) This was by clear design. My sole objective entering into this process was to be *completely* free and at peace with food. I was determined to find the way to obtain and maintain my ideal, naturally lean body weight in absolutely *any* situation, without dieting or willpower—and *with* my sanity. (Tall order!) If getting or staying thin was somehow dependent on my exercising to burn excess calories that would have put my desired outcome at the precarious mercy of my (then non-existent) willpower. This would not do. Therefore, I needed my solution not to be tied to, or any way dependent upon, exercise.

Just as I arrived at eating consistently healthier than I ever imagined as the result of a journey that began with Donuts and Doritos, I created an inside-out irresistible love for exercise (and *real, visible* muscles on my body!) by initially completely eliminating it. At seventeen, I moved to Los Angeles for college and promptly developed a shaky and chaotic relationship with exercise. I fancied it my secret weapon (torture device) to repair the caloric damage from my then out of control Non-Hunger Eating. But in truth, I was its servant. And with my glaring lack of willpower at that time—I was not a very good one at that.

So at the beginning of my quest for a peace with food solution—the same week I went on the aforementioned eat-what-you-really-want-stock-the-cupboards-with-every-thing-you've-ever-forbidden-birthday-sheetcake-inclusive grocery spree—I completely stopped formal exercise. It was terrifying. I had a circus of chatter going through my head that I'd be unhealthy and (far more important to my weight-obsessed mind at that time) *not* lean. But I knew it was *vital* that I disconnect exercise from my weight. At that time, when I would formally exercise it triggered that old diet thinking, I'd count the calories burned on the treadmill, and my eating would go haywire. So, I took the leap and decided to stop all formal exercise and focused on Hunger Directed Eating. And I lost weight. *A lot* of weight. It was the precise liberation I needed from diet-logic at that time to see myself swiftly slimming without doing any "gym" type of exercise. I had finally pulled the destructive connection between exercise and burning calories for weight loss out of my life by its root.

My current daily-ish peaceful but invigorating relationship with exercise sprouted from an entirely different seed. While I was mastering Hunger Directed Eating I worked ardently at identifying and amassing the tools required to replace Emotional Eating with more productive coping responses. My research on the mood-boosting impact of exercise led me to experiment with physical activity as the equivalent of an "optimism pill." Since my objective had *nothing* whatsoever to do with burning calories, I set myself up for optimum success because I was then able to borrow from another Japanese engineering principal—Kaizen. Kaizen is the concept of creating monumental strides by making *very* small continuous improvements. Going big by starting small.

When I was "diet-girl," I'd need to run for an hour or five miles for a workout to count (or even be worth it). Now that I was exploring the psychological effects of exercise, things looked very different. I created a specific cognitive technique that enabled me to generate the same pull toward exercise that I had previously felt for snack cakes. (I know… crazy, *right*?! I'll teach you how to do this below!) I began taking ten-minute walks. Not in workout clothes and sneakers—in my pencil skirts and wedge-heeled strappy sandals. I wouldn't walk the track. I'd walk from Starbucks to Sephora. And not every day. Just when I felt like it. I would then measure the specific changes in my mood and energy. These short walks paired with the measurement process seismically shifted exercise from a grueling *Should* to a full-fledged, inside-out, powerful, emphatic *Want To.* I now eagerly move my body and raise my heart rate in some way, shape, or form almost every day—because I genuinely *want* to. I want to take a walk or do pushups the same way I really want to brush my teeth in the morning. They are both things I am certain will make me feel great. (And if not "great" *every* time—at least a heck of lot better than if I didn't!)

So by quitting exercise altogether I now for the first time in my adult life am someone with actual muscles on her arms, abs, and thighs. I'm not saying I'm a fitness model *by any measure.* But hey, when I wave to a friend, now my *entire* arm stops moving at the same time—it's the little things in life.

HOW TO FALL IN LOVE WITH EXERCISE

So let me be clear. Exercise is indisputably one of the *most beneficial activities* you can choose to do. It relieves tension, depression, and anxiety. It boosts your mood, energy, overall health, bone density, and ability to focus. And the list goes on. And on. But I'm guessing that you already know this. If exercise is in the *Should* category where you dread it—but know it's good for you and therefore think you should do it—all the research in the world isn't going to spring you up out of your seat with unbridled enthusiasm to go for a walk. There *are* however a few small cognitive tweaks you can easily make to the way you think about exercise that might do just that. (But again, just to be crystal clear, this is only to gain the *true* benefits of exercise, not a smoke and mirrors technique to "trick" yourself into burning calories for weight loss.)

So, let's look at *how* you can reap all these benefits of exercise without landing you in the Krispy Kreme drive-thru. By taking exercise out of the weight loss equation (where it isn't needed *or effective* anyway) and putting it back into its natural place—of making you think clearly and look and feel vibrant—you pop it out of the grueling *Should* category. Which is essential, since it puts you at high risk for boomerang eating and feeling like you need a (food) reward, and moves it over into the *Want To* spot, where exercising itself is the reward!

1. Breaking the Connection between Exercise and Burning Calories

It's very likely that in your mind (up to this point) diet and exercise has always seemed to go together, like… peanut butter and jelly. It makes perfect sense that you'd believe exercise is essential for weight loss. This little bit of diet-lore has been pummeled into your head for years. Every diet book, talk show, and women's magazine touts the magic weight loss formula: limit your calories + exercise = (*voila*) promised lasting weight loss. Except for the pesky little fact that it's *not* working. Right?

As the previous study illustrates, exercising for the purpose of creating a calorie deficit backfires. So if your relationship with exercise could use an overhaul, the first step in creating a more satisfying connection is to *completely* disconnect the act of moving your body (exercising) from burning calories and weight loss. (It is *so* liberating!)

2. Exercise Will Make You Happier–*Guaranteed*

Exercise is the closest thing to a magic "happy pill" this world has to offer. It's been clinically proven time and time again to be as effective as prescription antidepressants for eliminating depression—with none of the horrific side effects! Sonja Lyubomirsky, a forerunner in the research on happiness, makes this uncharacteristically bold claim about exercise, "No one in our society needs to be told that exercise is good for us… But has anyone told you—indeed, guaranteed you—that regular physical activity will make you happier? I swear by it." This is a woman who dedicates her life to scientifically examining the factors that make people happy.

But here's the thing. I can quote a zillion studies and show you volumes of empirical evidence that exercise will make you feel amazing, but the only way it can truly transform from a *Should* to a *Want To* is by your own little piece of experiential research.

The 10-Minute 10,000 Calorie Sparing Miracle

Okay, so if I told you there was one thing you could do in just *ten real clock minutes* that would spare you thousands of calories, make you happy, and solve the majority of your current problems—would you be willing to give it a try? As an undergraduate

I had the great fortune to study under renowned mood expert Dr. Robert Thayer, Ph.D., who is well known for his studies comparing the mood impact of a ten-minute walk with that of a candy bar. Participants would take a ten-minute brisk walk on one day and eat a candy bar on another. They would fill out a mood assessment both before and at various points after the walk or the candy. Not surprisingly, Thayer found that initially the candy bar would cause their energy to spike, shooting up much higher than it was before they ate the candy. But half an hour later that heightened energy level would precipitously plunge to lower than it was *before* they ate the bar. Their tension was also higher than before the candy snack. Whereas when they took the ten-minute brisk walk, they enjoyed sustained higher energy *and* lower tension for up to three hours after their brief jaunt. And we aren't talking about an intensive gym-clothes-required workout here. No, Dr. Thayer found that simply walking as fast as you would if you were late for a movie you really wanted to see was all you needed to obtain the instant mood-boosting effects.

But wait, there's more. (And *finally,* in a good way!) Thayer's later studies found that this same ten-minute walk had a dramatic impact on how people viewed their problems. People rated their most stressful problems as *significantly more solvable* after just ten minutes of walking. Okay, so they not only had more energy, less tension, and were in a better mood—but they saw their most troubling problems as more solvable. *After just 10 minutes of walking.* One short brisk walk was enough to change their cognitive state so dramatically that the very same problem that may have seemed insurmountable as they headed out the door became significantly more manageable.

As we've discussed, Emotional Eating has the singular aim of changing the way we're feeling. The problem is, although it may work in the moment, in the long run it actually creates more bad feelings. Imagine *wanting* to turn to something that actually helped in the moment—and afterwards. Just think of all the calories (and heartache) you could spare yourself in those high-stress moments if you could crave a walk the way you do a cupcake. Guess what. You can create that craving. Seriously! Here's how.

How to Crave a Walk More Than a Cupcake

Knowing intellectually that eating spinach and jogging are "good for you" does absolutely nothing to make you authentically crave them. (Although somehow this knowledge can still successfully make you feel guilty for *not* choosing to do them.) Outside-in information has no impact on our urges. Intellectual knowledge and experiential desire originate in very different regions of the brain. Dr. Thayer's research did change my life—but not until I experienced its benefits first-hand. It wasn't until a decade later when I experientially applied the one simple action that built the bridge between what I knew intellectually (walks boost your mood) and what I irresistibly wanted (to feel *better fast*): I took a ten-minute walk—to change the way I was feeling.

Our brains have a phenomenal built-in future-simulating device—the pre-frontal cortex. We have the unique ability to try on a scenario in our heads before we actually do it in real life. We do this all the time as a way to navigate our daily (and long-term) decisions. We can test drive something with our minds—*before* we buy. This is why, as Harvard psychologist Dan Gilbert explains, Ben and Jerry didn't need to whip up a batch of liver and onion ice cream in their test kitchen *before* deciding not to manufacture it. No, because without lifting a finger they could do a quick taste-test in their head using their pre-frontal cortex. All they would need to do is vividly imagine what liver and onions would taste (and smell) like mixed with sugar, egg, and smooth, velvety frozen cream. Ew, gross. But when they envision chocolate-covered pretzels in peanut butter ice cream... now that elicits a *completely* different response. Right?

You use your pre-frontal cortex *thousands* of times a day to make decisions. You mentally try an idea on—a movie or ice-skating tonight—and either nix it or carry it out depending on how it feels in your simulation. There are powerful ways you can make small adjustments to your cognitive test-run that dramatically impact the desirability of a given behavior. They are the basic building blocks of creating irresistible motivation. Once you master this skill you can *hand pick* whether an activity goes into the *Want To* or *Won't* category. Let's try it out with a walk and a cupcake.

My guess is that if exercise currently resides in your *Should* zone, when you hit that place where you're stressed and at the end of your rope, food sounds WAY more appealing than pounding it out at the gym. So if when you're wanting a fluffy, decadent, cream-cheese-frosted red velvet cupcake I suggested that you go for a walk instead (like so many *annoying* diet books do!)—well, truthfully, that's the point where 95% of us hurl the book across the room. (I've been there, *literally*.) But, if you *were* to run the idea of a walk through your future-simulator, you'd likely focus on how hard it would be to get up and muster the energy to go for a stroll. You'd probably think about how horribly sluggish and tired you feel and what an unwelcome, difficult demand it would be on you to take a walk right now—*SO* much effort. Then if you possibly even made it to imagining the first bit of walking, you'd be inclined only to register how boring and hard you *think* it would be. Thus, you'd (very understandably) ditch the idea of the walk—and go back to the cupcake.

When you think of the cupcake (or your go-to stress relief food of choice), you run an entirely different process through your prefrontal-cortex future-simulator than you do with the walk. With the walk, you imagined (and consequently felt in that moment) the painful emotions of transitioning into it, whereas with the tempting stress-release cupcake preview, you only associate the immense pleasure it will bring... *conveniently* leaving out how crummy you actually feel shortly afterwards—*and* in the long run. Your future-simulator preview—for *Cupcake: The Irresistible Cure-All Wonder Treat*—likely goes a little something like this. First, you hold a mental image of the cupcake. The creamy frosting glistens and shimmers like a carefully lit glamour shot. Then you mentally try on eating it. You can almost feel the sweet cupcake-y flavor sparking your senses to life with that initial bite. How rich it tastes, how fluffy and tender it is in your mouth. How happy and exhilarated you feel. You nail it as an effective marketer for that cupcake—and you have just built a truly *brilliant* marketing campaign for convincing yourself to eat it!

The great news is, you can take that compelling ad campaign that you already create in your mind—for wanting food when you're *not* hungry—and apply that same process to walking. (Or, for that matter, to *anything* else you want to do.) So the difference between the two commercials you just ran is that the cupcake advert focuses on the pleasure *and* (importantly) creates a palpable connection to that pleasure—yum! Whereas, the walk commercial focused on the pain of the behavior—yuck! But the truth is, if you're eating one (or five) when you're not hungry, that cupcake actually has much *more* potential pain (as we're all probably far too familiar with) than the walk does. It's just that the disappointment and/or actual discomfort you feel afterwards, or the frustration (or despair) you experience in the dressing room, is either *left out* of or *disregarded* from the decision-making process.

There is just as much, if not more, legitimate, lasting (and tantalizing) pleasure to be had from a walk. You've just been hyping that delectably frosted, couture cupcake for so long that you've already been convinced of only its (false) positives. So, it makes total sense that since you *don't* currently have access to the walk's pleasure points in the future-simulation phase, it's not going to hold a candle to the stress-relieving option of eating the cupcake. But thankfully, you can completely change that. Try this out. The next time you go on a walk, when you hit that endorphin release where your heart is beating and you feel vibrant, alert, alive, and as if your problems have all just shrunk in the dryer, consciously anchor *those* splendid sensations to walking. Do that just a handful of times—and you will have leveled the playing field. Just a couple times is enough to start shifting the balance. Because you're anchoring to something that *really* makes you feel good—both now *and* later— you'll be pleasantly surprised by how fast your mind makes this adjustment. Then the next time you're stressed and you mentally try on solutions, you will have the energy-boosting, invigorating (guilt-free) walk as a proven competitive alternative to the cupcake. And, *that is how you can spare yourself thousands of extra calories in just ten minutes.*

So here's a little tool you can use to help build the same internal pull for the walk as you have for the cupcake. The next time you hit a wall and feel stressed or stuck, or you're hearing the siren song of your favorite bakery, grab a piece of paper (or the notepad on your phone) and rate your mood. Focus on the following four variables—and give them a one to five rating.

> **Energy:** *One* – You're tired, lethargic, you can't go on. *Five* – You're bursting with energy, and feel completely invigorated, you're ready to take on the world.
>
> **Mood:** *One* – You're feeling really low, and totally bummed out. *Five* – You're elated, everything's possible.
>
> **Tension:** *One* – You're tightly wound and stressed out over your current problem/stressor. *Five* – You're loose, calm, and relaxed.
>
> **Problem Solvability:** *One* – Your self-talk sounds like, "I'm stuck. I'm going to be here forever. It's insurmountable." *Five* – Your self-talk sounds like, "I got this. Slam dunk. This is *totally* solvable."

Then, throw on your shoes (any shoes, no tennis shoes required!) and your headphones and head out the door. You could listen to music or your favorite motivational audiobook. Set a timer on your phone for ten minutes, and simply put one foot in front of the other. Just the speed you would if you were late to meet a girlfriend for coffee. Then, when the timer goes off, quickly pull out the same notepad and once again rate, one to five, where you are on your energy, mood, tension, and solvability of that problem you left behind. It is *amazing* to see the difference in your scores *just ten minutes* later. This concrete measurement of your before and (very shortly) after ratings builds a strong link from the inside-out between walking and how amazing it makes you feel. And before you know it, when you think of exercising you'll have an alive, alert, and refreshed feeling anchored to the activity. Your instant mood booster. It will become a new, win-win (good now *and* good later) coping mechanism for you—even *better* than a cupcake.

Now, between clients, if I hit a wall writing, or if I just have that funky anxiety feeling, I pop out the door and in about three to five minutes I usually have no idea why I even started walking. And, if you let it grow from the *inside out*, you'll give yourself the space to discover and notice the movements and types of exercise you genuinely love. So now with the majority of my girlfriends, we'll still get coffee or tea, but we'll also go for a walk around a nearby gorgeous lake or reservoir, or through a local shopping district. Not because we want to burn calories, but because we feel so much more engaged and energized when we're talking and walking.

3. Working Out and Grooming Your Eyebrows: Exercise as Part of Your Beauty Regimen

The third change to the way you classify working out is to think of toning exercises the same way you'd think about plucking or waxing your brows—as part of your beauty regimen. (OK, and for those of you far less superficial than me, this *also* works if you put it in your overall-strength-and-bone-density-boosting health routine category.)

In addition to supplying you with an instant mood boost, exercise can give you those firm, uplifted, pretty, pretty muscles. So after disconnecting working out from burning calories—and creating the new association to cardio (walking, running, skipping) that anchored its powerful ability to quickly and radically change your mood—I moved toning, weightlifting, and isometric types of exercises into the vanity part of my brain. Right next to painting my nails, waxing my brows, or better yet, shaving my legs—since like exercise, that also improves the way I look in a bikini.

LOVE STORY, THE SEQUEL: LEANING OUT AND FIRMING UP

So, even though at the end of my weight loss journey with Hunger Directed Eating I was lean—and wearing a size I never even fathomed—I noticed that some "things" still didn't quite sit where I'd like them to. And then, thanks to Kelly Ripa, I discovered the power of isometric and weight-bearing exercise—and *completely* transformed the way my body looked.

After being turned on to it by Ms. Ripa, I started doing the Physique 57 workout. Not to lose weight, *or* to burn a single calorie. And to be shamefully honest, not even to be "healthy" (though health and vitality are *now* powerful motivators). Quite frankly, my driving force was the desire to give my rear a friendly hand up—to a perkier perch. This type of exercise completely transformed my body in the same way that waxing my brows turns my one thick Italian eyebrow into two. Within a week of doing the new routine I had a real, long, lean muscle starting to poke its little head up on my arm. This is something I hadn't *ever* had before. Back in my dieting days I used to exercise like crazy, but I was a loyal disciple of calorie-burning cardio—and it was an exclusive relationship. Two months into *this* routine—my body was unrecognizable. (It is important to note that the *only* thing that changed in my eating was that I was eating *more*, because I was burning more calories and therefore hungry more often.) My clothes fit so differently—and by different, I mean better—and for the first time ever I started to see thigh and ab lines. (Ab lines! Are you kidding me?) But all vanity aside, the ability to physically transform my body (which I had spent decades battling) had a profound psychological impact on my sense of self-efficacy.

EXERCISE HAS TO BE FUN—OR FORGET IT!

It is extremely important that you keep exercise in the fun *Want To* category, and prevent it from becoming a grind where you *have to* go to the gym. So, if you do *choose* to exercise it is imperative that you set it up to be fun. When I started doing Physique 57 I did it with my neighbor Jessica, who I love. She would come over and our workout would be our time to connect and crack up. I refused to make exercise something I dreaded or forced myself to do.

I still stand by what I said at the beginning of this chapter. No, you absolutely do *not* need to exercise to get to and stay at your naturally thin weight. But when you change the way you think about exercise—and anchor the instant energy and mood-boosting benefits it creates—you'll likely find yourself eagerly desiring to get your body moving. So I invite you to consider separating exercise from weight loss and thinking about it as an instant mood fixing, muscle building, energy boosting, problem-solving panacea. Giving your mood and your bum a lift at the same time—now *that* is effective multi-tasking.

CALL ME!

So, we're at the end of the book and the beginning of your new ability to peacefully and freely relate to food. (And I have to admit—I'm going to miss you!) I want to send you off with this: You absolutely can make peace with food, get to and stay at your naturally thin weight, and get on with your exciting life. I see it every day with my clients and people just like you around the world who've read this book. It is exhilarating. Dieting is a faulty tool. You now have the right tool. Your naturally thin life awaits you. I encourage you to remember the toddler learning to walk and extend yourself the same tenderness and patience as you build your mastery with Hunger Directed Eating. With a little practice, Gasping for Food will be a distant memory. You can do this. I get scads of emails every week from women just like you, who feared they would never be able to ditch dieting and be thin and now are elated that they really can have their cake and their skinny jeans too.

To get updates on the strategies to eliminate emotional eating, share an exciting discovery you've made along your journey, or to find out more about individual coaching (with me), drop me a line. I'd love to hear from you!

Website: www.JosieSpinardi.com
Twitter: @JosieSpinardi
Instagram: @JosieSpinardi
Until next time…

SPREAD THE WORD!

I hope you loved this book! If you found it helpful, eye-opening or enjoyable and you'd like to help get this message into the hands of other women who hurt with food—there is something you can do.

Please take a quick moment to go to Amazon and leave a review. (It doesn't have to be long or billowy. Or even use complete sentences! No. Really.)

We as women rely on each other's valuable opinions before we make important decisions. Reviews by readers make a huge difference in getting information into the hands of a reader who needs it.

Your feedback is incredibly helpful to women out there who are ready to make a change in their painful relationship with food and aren't quite sure where to turn. You really can make a difference in their lives.

Thank you!

Josie

ACKNOWLEDGMENTS

Dedication

This book is dedicated to my amazing Thin-Coaching clients and readers. Thank you for your constant supply of kind words, brave transparency and being with me on the other side of the screen and page.

In most affectionate memory of my wonderful father, who sagaciously introduced me to cognitive psychology when I was five and saved everything I've ever written since the third grade in his desk drawer. Thank you for believing in me.

A Huge Thank You

Miabella, for being incandescently, joyfully you. Taryn, Erika & Jessica, you are the Amex Black Card of friendship. Mom, for making me take that dreaded typing class in the 9th grade. You were right. Tuck, for existing in consummate list form and for the steady supply of duct tape and singularity. Women's World Magazine for naming me "America's Ultimate Expert in Emotional Eating."

Elly, there are not enough words (not my usual challenge!) to express my gratitude for all you have brought to this project. Supermodels get Photoshop to make them look good, a writer—if she's lucky—gets a brilliant, insightful (and fun!) editor like Elly Milder. Thank you Sarah McCarry, Leah Gordon, Adam Tervort and Sherry Heinitz for lending your genius to this work. Marcy Atoigue, thank you for changing the lives of children with dyslexia, miraculously transforming them into thriving readers—your technique is equal parts genius and magic.

And above all, thank *you*, fabulous brave reader, for opening this book—and your mind to the possibility that your life can be dramatically different. And by different, *I mean better*. You absolutely can make peace with food, get (and stay!) thin and get on with your wondrous life!

CPSIA information can be obtained at www.ICGtesting.com
Printed in the USA
LVOW07s0149020916

502890LV00013B/130/P

9 780988 954410